THE
MAN
CITY
MISCELLANY

THE
MAN
CITY

MISCELLANY

DAVID CLAYTON

FOREWORD BY SHAUN GOATER

*For my cousin, Don Roberts, fearless custodian of
AFC Ladybarn Villa, circa 1977–9, unbeaten(ish) in all
four games played at the Croft Stadium, Ladybarn Lane.*

First published in 2007 by Sutton Publishing
This new and revised edition published in 2011 by

The History Press
The Mill, Brimscombe Port
Stroud, Gloucestershire, GL5 2QG
www.thehistorypress.co.uk

British Library Cataloguing in Publication Data.
A catalogue record for this book is available from the British Library.

ISBN 978 0 7524 6373 5

Typesetting and origination by The History Press
Printed in the EU for The History Press.

FOREWORD

There are a million and one things about Manchester City that could fill 10 volumes of miscellanies, but I think David Clayton has picked out the best for this book. Having enjoyed so many great years playing for the club, it was fascinating to flick through the pages and learn things I'd never known about City, but as a footballer, you're paid to go out and try to become part of history rather than study what's happened in the years before you arrived.

You know the tradition and general history, but if you asked me detailed questions about the past, I'd struggle, as I think most people would. Now I've read this, I've no excuse not to know everything from the name of the club cat to what Clive Allen's dog was called and with the beautiful Bermudian sunshine to sit in, I think I'll swot up on the more pertinent facts and figures so I'm well prepared for my next visit to Manchester. Feed the Goat – with facts!

See you soon,

Shaun Goater, Bermuda

THE MISCELLANY

THEY SAID IT…

'John Bond has blackened my name with his insinuations about the private lives of football managers. Both my wives are upset.'

Malcolm Allison responds to press criticism from his successor at Maine Road (1980)

'The fans of Manchester City made me feel welcome from day one – everybody at the club did. Obviously I was thinking very carefully about the move – was it worth it to just go from one club to the other? But I'm delighted that I made the decision to join City. The biggest motivation is that City have put a lot of trust in myself – and for that I am very grateful.'

Carlos Tevez on the move from United to City

'No, no, no. We can't have him. Isn't he the lad who threw a bed out of the window at Lilleshall?'

Joe Mercer expresses doubt to Allison regarding 'bad-boy' Tony Coleman joining the Blues (1967)

'Richard Dunne has always been in the frame for me. When he has been out of the frame it was because he took himself out of it for one reason or another.'

Kevin Keegan, explaining something in a manner only Kevin Keegan could (circa 2002)

'I'm not trying to make excuses but I think the lights may have been a problem.'

Kevin Keegan tries to exonerate David Seaman error, unsuccessfully (2003)

'If anybody's offended by seeing a backside, get real. Maybe they're just jealous that he's got a real nice tight one, with no cellulite or anything. I thought his bum cheeks looked very pert.'

Ian Holloway lends his view of Joey Barton's decision to bare his backside to Everton fans (2006)

'It looks like the Lazio badge with that eagle on it. The last badge had a little ship on it going down the Manchester Ship Canal and the rose of Lancashire. When was the last time you saw an eagle in Manchester?'

Noel Gallagher, less than impressed by City's newly designed badge (1998)

'I think he's an absolutely fantastic bloke, top geezer, and if he wants to carry a little horse on the side of the pitch, I don't care!'

Ian Holloway on Stuart Pearce's lucky mascot 'Beanie'

'My biggest ambition is to win something in the shirt of City – not just for me but for all the players – we all want to win something. We want to break the years of nothing – to win and giving that happiness and ambition to the supporters. It's important not just to win one trophy, but to win several trophies and obviously – I don't just want to win one championship I want to win all the championships!'

Carlos Tevez

DERBY DAYS

The first Manchester derby, such as it was, took place on 3 October 1891 when Newton Heath beat Ardwick 5–1 in an FA Cup first round qualifier. The first competitive fixture the teams played as Manchester City v Manchester United was on Christmas Day 1902, when a record derby crowd of 40,000 witnessed a 1–1 draw at Old Trafford. United had the bragging rights in the return fixture at Hyde Road, winning 2–0. Owing to the Blues' promotion that season, City had to wait until 1 December 1906 to record a first league win over Manchester United, with a 3–0 win delighting the 30,000 Hyde Road crowd – well, most of them. In 2008 City ended a 34-year wait for a win at Old Trafford when goals from Darius Vassell and Benjani secured a rare 2–1 win.

The complete record is:

League	Pld	W	D	L	F	A
City	144	39	49	56	190	212
United	144	56	49	39	212	190
FA Cup						
City	7	2	0	5	5	9
United	7	5	0	2	9	5
League Cup						
City	5	3	1	1	12	6
United	5	1	1	3	6	12
Charity Shield						
City	1	0	0	1	0	1
United	1	1	0	0	1	0
Totals	Pld	W	D	L	F	A
City	157	42	50	62	207	228
United	157	62	50	42	228	207

I'VE STARTED ... BUT I WON'T FINISH

A total of 19 matches have failed to reach a natural end over the years, abandoned by the official for one reason or another. Incredibly, City were losing in only one of those games. There have been several particularly galling halts to proceedings, but none more so than the time Denis Law, a raw but deadly young striker fresh from Huddersfield Town, scored a double hat-trick – yes, six goals – as City ran riot away to Luton Town. Leading 6–2 with only 69 minutes on the clock, the muddy conditions became unplayable and referee Ken Tuck decided to end Luton's misery by abandoning the game. The home players and fans went home breathing a huge sigh of relief – when they had dried out – but how young Law must have rued his misfortune after such an awesome display of finishing! The replay saw City lose 3–1, with Law scoring again but watching the team he'd bagged seven against progress into the next round.

Only two games since 1969 have been abandoned and have both been against the same club – Ipswich Town. Excess surface water was the reason each match ended before the 90 minutes were up. The first occasion, in 1994, saw City leading 2–0 in a crucial Premiership game and the decision understandably infuriated the home fans. Fortunately, the Blues won the replayed match 2–1. Then, in December 2000, Paul Dickov clawed City level in a Worthington Cup tie with the same opponents. Referee Graham Poll had seen enough and, with the water almost ankle-deep, took the players off. This time, Ipswich were the victors when the tie was rearranged, winning the game 2–1 in extra time.

The total record for how the abandoned games stood is:
Winning: 5   Drawing: 13   Losing: 1   For: 23   Against: 12

The record for the rearranged fixtures is:
Won: 10   Drawn: 3   Lost: 6   For: 25   Against: 23

THEY SAID IT...

'I felt like I had a mountain to climb to prove myself. But I didn't mind that – I was up for the challenge and I like turning up for training every day really hungry. The gaffer had a big squad and he was just finding everybody out. There were a lot of people in the same category as me. But I knew from the way I was training and the way I performed in friendlies that it was just a matter of time.'

2008/09 Player of the Year Stephen Ireland

'We are at a point in time where there are four very strong clubs in English football. But we had a point in time when they thought the four-minute mile could not be broken. What we have to do is develop an investment plan and a strategy to change that.'

MCFC Chief Executive, Garry Cook

ACADEMY

In 1998, the Blues launched the Manchester City Academy, based close to the club's former Maine Road stadium at Platt Lane. A more professional set-up with strict criteria set by various organisations, the main focus was to coach as many young hopefuls through to the first team as possible.

In 2010, Ryan McGivern became the 36th youngster in 12 years to graduate from the Academy to play first-team football – an incredible achievement by Academy Director Jim Cassell and his coaches. Five of the graduates have gone on to win full caps for their country, too, with Shaun Wright-Phillips – the first player to go from the Academy into the senior side – Micah Richards and Joey Barton all playing for England, and Stephen Ireland and Stephen Elliot playing for Ireland. The full list of graduates who've played for the first team as of April 2010 is:

Barton, Joey
Boyata, Dedryck
Chantler, Chris
Croft, Lee
Cunningham, Greg
D'Laryea, Jon
Dunfield, Terry
Elliott, Stephen
Etuhu, Dickson
Etuhu, Kelvin
Evans, Ched
Flood, Willo
Guidetti, John
Ireland, Stephen
Johnson, Michael
Jordan, Stephen
Killen, Chris
Logan, Shaleum
McGivern, Ryan
Mears, Tyrone
Mee, Ben
Mike, Leon
Miller, Ishmael
Nimely-Tchuimeni, Alex

Onuoha, Nedum
Richards, Micah
Razak, Abdul
Schmeichel, Kasper
Shuker, Chris
Sturridge, Danny
Vidal, Javan
Weiss, Vladimir
Whelan, Glenn
Williamson, Sam
Wright-Phillips, Bradley
Wright-Phillips, Shaun

COMING TO AMERICA

The first players to quit City to play in the USA date back as far as 1894 when no less than four of the Blues' 1894/95 squad headed Stateside to play for Baltimore Orioles. M. Calvey played 7 games and scored 5 goals before he left; full-back A. Ferguson played just a couple of games; winger T. Little made 7 starts and scored 3 times and A. Wallace made 6 starts and scored once. They all left the club on 13 October to join English coach A.W. Stewart. Drawing over 8,000 to their opening home game, the Orioles seemed intent on duplicating the success of the Baltimore baseball club, who were the 1894 National League champions.

Baltimore established themselves as the league leaders but the other clubs were not amused at Baltimore's methods and after being thrashed by the Orioles 10–1, Washington Nationals coach Art Schmelz complained of the Baltimore club's use of British professionals. The press picked up on the story, and a full-blown controversy ensued. Baltimore, for its part, rather unconvincingly alleged that most of its players were from Detroit! Presumably the Mancunian accents suggested otherwise because the US Government announced its intention to investigate the Orioles' importation of British professionals. The league owners decided that the time had come to pull the plug on the venture. Thus, on 20 October, a mere 6 games into the season, the ALPF (American League of Professional Football) folded. It is not known whether the four former Blues remained in the States or returned home.

In 1924, M. Hamill quit Manchester for Boston's Fall River Marksmen, and, just like the quartet before them, he was part of a successful side as Fall River went on to win the American Soccer League. It was 44 years before the next Atlantic crossing – here is the full list of American dreamers:

Roy Cheetham	Detroit Cougars	1968
Rodney Marsh	Tampa Bay Rowdies	1975
Dennis Tueart	New York Cosmos	1978
Jimmy Conway	Portland Timbers	1978
Ron Futcher	Minnesota Kicks	1976
Willie Donachie	Portland Timbers	1980
Colin Bell	San Jose Earthquakes	1980
Steve Daley	Seattle Sounders	1981
Keith MacRae	Portland Timbers	1981
Nicky Reid	Seattle Sounders	1982
Joe Corrigan	Seattle Sounders	1983
Kaziu Deyna	San Diego Sockers	1981
Asa Hartford	Fort Lauderdale	1984
David Cross	Vancouver Whitecaps	1983
David Johnson	Tulsa Roughnecks	1984
Steve Kinsey	Minnesota Kicks	1986
Ian Bishop	Miami Fusion	2003

THEY SAID IT...

'Suddenly, I win the derby and people are talking about England again. It is absolutely pathetic.'
Stuart Pearce responds to the adulation poured on him after beating Man United 3–1 (2006)

'Sometimes we're good and sometimes we're bad but when we're good, at least we're much better than we used to be and when we are bad we're just as bad as we always used to be, so that's got to be good hasn't it?'
Mark Radcliffe, Radio 2 DJ & City fan (November 2001)

'Are you watching,
Are you watching,
Are you watching Macclesfield?'
City fans react to the Blues' relegation to Division Two with typical humour (May 1998)

'The fans are absolutely unbelievable at this club and I owe them so much.'
Gio Kinkladze (1997)

'The problem? I can't get the old boots on anymore and get out on the park and play. It would be a lot easier if I could.'
Francis Lee starts his tenure as City chairman with some trepidation (1994)

'I rang my secretary and asked "What time do we kick-off tonight?" and she said "Every ten minutes".'
Alan Ball finds even his staff have developed a gallows humour (1996)

UNLUCKY GROUNDS

You'll all no doubt know most of these off by heart – but here are the least fruitful venues for the Blues (to April 2007) since the Second World War:

1   **Highbury & Emirates**
    51 games, 32 defeats, 4 wins + 22 failures to score

2   **Anfield**
    46 games, 6 wins + 19 failures to score

3   **Portman Road**
    33 games, 21 defeats + 7 2–1 losses

4   **St James' Park**
    50 games, 29 defeats + 19 failures to score

5   **Ewood Park**
    28 games, 19 defeats + 11 losses in first 13 post-war visits

TOP 5 SEASON CURTAIN-RAISERS

There's nothing like getting off to a flyer – here's City's best opening-day victories to date:

1 v Bootle 7–0 (3 September 1892)
2 v Grimsby Town 7–2 (3 September 1898)
3 v Swansea Town 5–0 (27 August 1938)
4 v Bury 5–1 (1 September 1910)
5 v West Ham 4–0 (17 August 1974)

TOP 5 OPENING DAY NIGHTMARES

On the flipside, here are five opening fixtures to forget . . .

1 v Wolves 1–8 (18 August 1962)
2 v Preston 0–5 (21 August 1954)
3 v Wolves 1–5 (18 August 1956)
4 v Woolwich Arsenal 1–4 (1 September 1906)
5 v Charlton Athletic 0–4 (19 August 2000)

FIRST DAY FACT

Of the 61 opening matches City have played away from home, more than half have ended in either a victory or a draw.

MOST PLAYED OPENING DAY OPPONENTS

There are plenty of teams City have never met on the first day of the season having played just 51 different clubs. The Blues have, most notably, never met Bolton, Newcastle or Wigan and only played Manchester United once. Wolves, with seven meetings, and Liverpool, Sheffield Wednesday and Sunderland (all five apiece) are the most often-played opening day opponents. As for matches against teams from particular areas, the Midlands win with games against various clubs from the area.

NON-LEAGUE OPENERS

The only competitive game the Blues kicked off a season with, not including Charity Shield games, was against Total Network Solutions in August 2003. City won the UEFA Cup qualifying round match 5–0 and it was also the first competitive fixture held at the City of Manchester Stadium.

MARC-VIVIEN FOÉ – THE GENTLE GIANT

Marc-Vivien Foé signed for City following the 2002 World Cup in Japan and Korea. The Cameroon midfielder had been in impressive form for the Indomitable Lions and his addition to the Blues' engine room was a welcome boost to the club's return to the Premiership. The Blues paid £500,000 for his services and it would prove to be money extremely well spent. The tall, tough-tackling ball-winner chose the no. 23 shirt as his squad number and made his debut in the 3–0 opening-day defeat to Leeds United.

In the following months he became an important member of the first team and opened his scoring account for the club against Sunderland in December. It was the beginning of a prolific run of goals with 6 strikes coming within the space of just 23 days. His presence had become a driving force in midfield with his contribution enormous but he always went about his job quietly and for a hard man on the pitch, there were no face-to-face incidents with players from opposing clubs. He fought hard but fairly and was respected by his fellow professionals.

His scoring continued but he never sought the limelight and when he was interviewed he was keen to thank his team-mates' contribution and the City fans' backing – supporters he felt were amazing in their unswerving loyalty. He found the net again when City played Sunderland on 21 April but few realised that it would be the last goal ever scored at Maine Road, especially with two more home games to come.

By the end of the season he had scored 9 goals and finished second top scorer after Nicolas Anelka – quite a feat for a defensive midfielder and one that had won him an army of new fans at Maine Road. His popularity was often aired with the chant of 'Come on feed the Foé' – a variation of a Shaun Goater song.

Most expected City to make the deal permanent once the season finished but his club in France, Lyon, were demanding a fee of around £7 million which Kevin Keegan felt was unrealistic in the transfer climate at that time. Eventually, Lyon indicated that Foé could leave on a free transfer and it seemed the move to Manchester would at last become permanent. Negotiations were ongoing and despite interest from several other Premiership clubs, Foé's most likely destination was the club he had just spent a year on loan to.

The Confederations Cup began in France in June and Foé, wearing the no. 17 shirt he always wore for his country was instrumental in the Indomitable Lions reaching the semi-final. Though feeling unwell, he played for Cameroon against Colombia and during the game, tragically collapsed and died shortly after. Investigations into his untimely death revealed it was natural causes that brought an end to his life, but for the world of football and City fans in particular, it was unbelievable that this fit, powerful 28-year-old man should suffer such a fate.

Tributes poured in from around the world and City's old ground Maine Road became a shrine of flowers, flags, scarves and shirts from all over Britain and beyond. Marc-Vivien Foé was a much-loved man and a highly respected footballer. City have since removed his no. 23 shirt as a permanent mark of respect and further tributes are planned. His presence both on and off the pitch will be sorely missed.

AGE CONCERNS

Glyn Pardoe still holds the current club record for being the youngest player to play first-team football for City. He made his debut aged 15 years and 314 days old on 11 April 1962 and he went on to play a total of 374 times for the club. The oldest player to turn out was the legendary Billy Meredith, who was just 120 days short of his 50th birthday when City played Newcastle in a 1924 FA Cup semi-final. Micah Richards became the youngest defender to play for England when he won his first cap aged 18 in 2006.

TWO-LEGGED BEASTS

The highest aggregate scores for City in cup competitions, both domestic and European, are as follows:

League Cup

9–1 Notts County (1998/99) 1st leg: (a) 2–0 2nd leg: (h) 7–1
6–0 Torquay Utd (1983/84) 1st leg: (h) 6–0 2nd leg: (a) 0–0
6–0 Burnley (1999/2000) 1st leg: (h) 5–0 2nd leg: (a) 1–0

Division Two play-off semi-final

2–1 Wigan Athletic (1998/99) 1st leg: (a) 1–1 2nd leg: (h) 1–0

European Cup Winners' Cup

8–0 SK Lierse (1969/70) 1st leg: (a) 3–0 2nd leg: (h) 5–0

UEFA/Europa Cup

7–0 TNS (2003/04) 1st leg: (h) 5–0 2nd leg: (a) 2–0

Full Members' Cup

3–2 Hull City (1985/86) 1st leg: (a) 1–2 2nd leg: (h) 2–0

WELSH RARE BIT

City are one of a handful of teams to have played the Millennium Stadium in Cardiff, won, but not left with a trophy of some kind. The Blues played the second leg of a UEFA Cup qualifying round against Total Network Solutions at the home of Welsh football because TNS's venue was too small. City won 2–0 and that game, played in 2003, remains the Blues' only appearance there.

CHAMPERS AND CIGARS

Allison, Malcolm
Manager from 1972 to 1973 and 1979 to 1980
League Record: Pld: 83 W: 23 D: 25 L: 35 F: 96 A: 137

In July 1965, City manager Joe Mercer approached upcoming Plymouth Argyle boss Malcolm Allison and offered him the position of head coach at Maine Road. He accepted and so began one of the most successful management teams English football has ever seen. 'Genial Joe' and 'Big Mal' were a perfect match even though their personalities were like chalk and cheese. In their first season together they steered the Blues to the Second Division Championship and two years later, it was the First Division Championship trophy being held aloft by skipper Tony Book.

Seldom, if ever, had a club's fortunes been turned around in such dramatic fashion and there was much more to come. He was constantly being chased by other clubs and was linked with Leeds, Juventus and Coventry City before in 1972 he was offered the job he most coveted – manager of Manchester City. Allison felt he deserved more than just being coach, and after Joe Mercer left for Coventry, he was given his chance.

Yet, nine months down the line, City's flamboyant champagne-drinking, cigar-smoking manager had left for Crystal Palace – fedora and all. Believing he could no longer motivate the City players, he decided enough was enough and returned to his hometown of London. In July 1979, he returned to Maine Road for a second spell that was nothing short of a disaster.

He tore the heart out of a side that had consistently challenged for Europe throughout the 1970s and replaced them with an assortment of teenagers, unknowns and million-pound flops. In October 1980, Allison was sacked and in Groundhog Day circumstances, returned to Crystal Palace. It would be his last high-profile job in English football. Allison, once said: 'I used to shout that I was the greatest coach in the world.' Few, especially the players who played under him in the late 1960s, would disagree.

Sadly, Malcolm died in 2010 after many years of failing health – the City fans gave him a minute's applause as a mark of respect.

BLOODY AMATEURS!

A total of 11 players have represented City while still at amateur status. The most famous in the list is legendary winger Billy Meredith, who turned professional after three months of the 1894/95 season. Sam Ashworth is one of only three amateurs to collect a FA Cup Winners' medal after City beat Bolton Wanderers 1–0 in the 1904 final. The full list is:

Billy Meredith	1894/95
Sam Ashworth	1903/04
Horace Blew	1906/07
John Willy Swann	1909–12
George Webb	1912/13
John Brennan	1914–22
Stan Royle	1917–22
Max Woosnam	1919–25
Jim Mitchell	1922–6
Derek Williams	1951–5
Phil Woosnam	1951–4

PASTA MASTERS?

The Anglo-Italian Cup: City played in this bizarre competition on only one occasion. In September 1970, the winners of the League Cup met the winners of the Italian Cup on a two-legged basis and the Blues played Bologna away in the first leg, losing 1–0 in front of a 28,000 crowd. The return leg ended in a 2–2 draw at Maine Road in front of a respectable 25,843 fans and that was the sum total of the Blues' involvement. Travel costs and poor crowds eventually saw the demise of the cup but it did make a brief reappearance a few years back, only to encounter the same difficulties as before – and the Intertoto Cup gets bad press!

GREAT SCOTS!

The Anglo-Scottish Cup was little more than a pre-season warm-up for the majority of clubs involved and particularly for the Blues. Formerly known as the Texaco Cup, it consisted of three group games with the winners meeting Scottish opposition. City lost 1–0 to both Blackpool and Blackburn and beat Sheffield United 3–1 at Maine Road, failing to qualify. Therefore, City never actually met Scottish opposition and never have in any competition to this day – unless you include the pre-season tournament the Tennents-Caledonian Cup in 1976, when the Blues beat Partick Thistle 4–1 – does that count? You decide.

KEEPING UP APPEARANCES:

All-time City record appearance holders:

	Player & Position	Duration	Apps	Sub	Gls
1	Alan Oakes (HB)	1958–76	665	4	34
2	Joe Corrigan (GK)	1966–83	592	0	0
3	Mike Doyle (HB)	1962–78	551	7	40
4	Bert Trautmann (GK)	1949–64	545	0	0
5	Eric Brook (W)	1928–40	494	0	178
6	Colin Bell (MF)	1966–79	489	3	152
7	Tommy Booth (CB)	1965–81	476	4	36
8	Mike Summerbee (F)	1965–75	441	2	67
9	Paul Power (MF)	1973–86	430	9	35
10	Willie Donachie (FB)	1968–80	421	5	2

BOXING DAY FACT

There were 69 days between fixtures in season 1962/63 owing to a terrible winter that left the country under several feet of snow and ice-bound. City played Wolves on 15 December and drew 3–3, but there was no Christmas period to warm the cockles as the rest of the month was wiped out and all of January was cancelled. The fixtures didn't resume until the Blues drew 1–1 with Leyton Orient on 23 February – technically an unbeaten run of three months!

CLOCKING UP APPEARANCES

Legendary goalie Joe Corrigan holds the record for consecutive appearances after starting 198 league games without a break between 8 November 1975 and 23 August 1980. Frank Swift made 195 successive appearances following his debut and winger Eric Brook made 165 consecutive senior starts between November 1929 and October 1933. Steve Redmond, Eric Westwood, Alex Williams and Billy 'Spud' Murphy have all cleared 100 without missing a match and Joe Fagan clocked up 121 successive games.

AND ON THE EIGHTH DAY ...

When the skipper of Gorton Football Club, a sturdy lad by the name of McKenzie, discovered an ideal patch of ground for his team to make their home on, they upped sticks and moved lock, stock and barrel to Ardwick. It was agreed that it made sense to change the name from Gorton FC to Ardwick FC and so a new club was formed. Consequently, the profile of the team began to rise. The League was still in its embryonic stages and teams appeared and disappeared at an alarming but understandable rate. Ardwick twice won the Manchester Cup, beating Newton Heath 1–0 in 1891, who were soon to become cross-town rivals Manchester United. Beset by financial problems, in 1893/94 the club was forced into bankruptcy and in 1894 the phoenix that arose from the ashes of Ardwick FC was Manchester City Football Club. City would continue to play in Ardwick until 1923, at Hyde Road.

THE MAINE MEN

In terms of trophies, promotions and win ratios, these are City's most successful managers:

Joe Mercer: 1965–71
Trophies: Old Division Two Champions 1966; Old Division One Champions 1968; FA Cup 1969; League Cup 1970; European Cup Winners' Cup 1970
Highest League position: Champions Old Division One, 1966
Promotions: 1 – 1966
Relegations: 0
Overall record:
Pld: 340 (League 263) W: 149 D: 94 L: 97 F: 526 A: 366

Wilfred Wild: 1932–46, 1947*
Trophies: FA Cup 1934; Division One Champions 1937
Highest League position: Champions Old Division One
Promotions: 0
Relegations: 1 – 1938
Overall record:
Pld: 628 (League 332) W: 288 D: 120 L: 220 F: 1336 A: 1053
*(including caretaker)

Les McDowall: 1950–63
Trophies: FA Cup 1956
Highest League position: Runners-up Old Division One 1951
Promotions: 1 – 1951
Relegations: 1 – 1963
Overall record:
Pld: 592 (League 546) W: 220 D: 127 L: 245 F: 1049 A: 1136

Tony Book: 1974–9
Trophies: League Cup 1976
Highest league position: Runners-up Old Division One 1977
Promotions: 0
Relegations: 0
Overall record:
Pld: 274 (League 219) W: 114 D: 76   L: 84   F: 411   A: 320*
*(includes caretaker)

Joe Royle: 1998–2001
Trophies: none
Highest League position: Runners-up Old Division Two 2000
Promotions: 2 – 1999, 2000
Relegations: 2 – 1998, 2001
Overall record:
Pld: 171 (League 145) W: 74   D: 46   L: 51   F: 261   A: 192

FOOTBALL KITTY

City's Club Cat was bizarrely christened 'Wimblydon' by former conditioning coach Juan Carlos Osorio. Shortly after the Blues moved training grounds to Carrington, a white and ginger stray started visiting, looking for the odd scrap of food and a saucer of milk. While 'Puss' was initially the popular moniker, when Osorio mentioned in his South American accent that City were playing 'Wimblydon' the next day, the faithful moggy appeared shortly after the laughter died down and so his legend was born. Wimblydon once offered a dead mouse outside Kevin Keegan's office – perhaps a gift or maybe his way of saying he didn't think much of the football on offer. By April 2010, Wimbly was still visiting the main reception for his daily feeds.

PACKED IN LIKE SARDINES, APPARENTLY

City still hold the provincial record for the biggest crowd in a competitive English match. An amazing 84,569 people crammed into Maine Road to see City beat Stoke 1–0 in a 1934 FA Cup tie. It was 26,000 higher than any League game that season and the Blues went all the way to Wembley, beating Portsmouth 2–1 to lift the trophy.

Ten years earlier, City's new home was packed with 76,166 fans to watch City draw 0–0 with Cardiff City. As late as 1956, two crowds of 76,129 and 70,640 watched the Blues take on Everton and Liverpool respectively in the FA Cup. City would win the trophy that season, having no doubt been buoyed by the tremendous support they were receiving. The record League crowd is 79,491 against Arsenal in February 1935 with the Gunners holding out for a 1–1 draw. The lowest crowd on record is 3,000 in 1924 when Nottingham Forest were the visitors and they took full advantage of the depressing atmosphere by beating City 3–1. Only 8,015 attended a Second Division clash with Swindon Town in 1964. Manchester United may keep adding seats to Old Trafford, but they are still around 8,000 shy of beating the Blues' attendance record.

WIZARDS OF OZ

City have had several connections with Australia over the years. Danny Tiatto became the first Australian to play for City and after a slow start to his career, the utility man and former Blues Player of the Year 2000/01 became a huge hit with the fans. Striker Danny Allsopp was signed from his hometown team Melbourne Sharks in 1998 and Simon Colosimo played a couple of games for the club during 2001 before being released. The Australian national team toured in November 1984 and a sparse crowd watched them beat City 3–1 at Maine Road. Fourteen years earlier, in 1970, Australia went down 2–0 to the Blues as they visited Maine Road for the first time. The year before, City had toured Down Under for the only time, winning six and drawing one of their unbeaten month-long tour. There are several City supporters' branches in Australia, too.

WE'RE REALLY NOT HERE ...

City entered the Auto Windscreens Trophy in 1998 and their record in this competition is easy enough to remember: played one, lost one. Arguably the lowest point in the club's history, City played Mansfield Town at Maine Road and lost 2–1 in front of barely 3,000 fans. The game itself was unimportant and the trophy meant nothing to City fans; most of them saw it as little more than an embarrassment, which showed how far the team had slipped since the glory days of the late 1960s.

ROAD TRIP

Best Away Wins:
9–3 v Tranmere Rovers (26 December 1938) Division Two
7–0 v Reading (31 January 1968) FA Cup third round (replay)
7–1 v Derby County (29 January 1938) Division One
6–0 v Burnley (9 March 1999) Division Two
6–1 v Burnley (4 April 2010) Premier League
6–1 v Wolves (21 March 1904) Division One
6–1 v Manchester United (23 January 1926) Division One
6–1 v Clapton Orient (6 March 1926) FA Cup sixth round

Worst Away Defeats:
2–10 v Small Heath (17 March 1894) Division Two
1–9 v Everton (3 September 1906) Division One
2–9 v West Brom (21 September 1957) Division One

Highest Scoring Draw:
4–4 v Chelsea (3 February 1937) Division One

Most away wins in a season: 12 in 2001/02 (Division One)
Fewest away wins in a season: 0 in 1986/87 (Division One)
Most away defeats in a season: 16 in 1958/59 (Division One)
Fewest away defeats in a season: 4 in 1898/99 and 1902/03 (both Division Two)
Most away goals in a season: 51 in 1936/37 (Division One)
Fewest away goals in a season: 8 in 1986/87 (Division One)

HAIR TODAY …

Bald players have been few and far between at Maine Road and looking back at shots of Bobby Charlton and Ralph Coates with their 1970s wraparounds hanging down one shoulder, we should thank God for small mercies. Basil Fawlty look-alike Barry Siddall (1985–6) and midfield hard man Steve McMahon (1991–5) were both thin on top, as was German full-back Michael Frontzeck (1995–7), but there just aren't that many bald players around these days. Back in the 1950s and '60s it seemed almost mandatory to have at least three or four in each side. Danny Mills, Ousmane Dabo, Trevor Sinclair and Nicolas Anelka have made the fashion popular again at City in recent(ish) years, with a mixture of balding pates and shaven heads, but oh, for those combovers of yesteryear. . . .

UNDER ORDERS

City's best start to a season was made at the beginning of 1914/15. City won 7 and drew 4 of their opening fixtures before Sheffield Wednesday turned party poopers with a 2–1 win over the Blues at Hillsborough. City finished fifth in Division One and would have probably won the League, but for an awful run-in of just 3 wins from the final 14 fixtures.

BOGEY TEAMS

City have had several 'bogey teams' over the years – indeed there have been times when it has seemed as though there were 91 of them! Wolves, Chelsea and particularly Tottenham have left Maine Road and the City of Manchester Stadium with maximum points on many occasions, while the Blues haven't won away to Arsenal since 1975. Wimbledon have proved a tough side for City – as emphasised during the 2001/02 season when the Dons won 4–0 in Manchester and then won the return 2–1, and in doing so became the only side to do the double over the eventual champions. Middlesbrough (up to season 2006/07 when City completed an almost unheard-of League double) and – wait for it – Stockport County and Wigan also seem to hold the Indian sign over the Blues, whereas Oldham Athletic rarely got beaten at Maine Road. Typical City!

GONE BUT FORGOTTEN – SHORTEST MANAGERIAL REIGNS & RECORDS

1. Steve Coppell: 1996
Lasted: 6 games
Won: 2   Drew: 1   Lost: 3   For: 7   Against: 10

2. John Benson: 1983
Lasted: 17 games.
Won: 3   Drew: 2   Lost: 12   For: 13   Against: 32

3. Johnny Hart: 1973
Lasted: 22 games.
Won: 11   Drew: 5   Lost: 6   For: 26   Against: 22

4. Ron Saunders: 1973/74
Lasted: 29 games.
Won: 9   Drew: 10   Lost: 10   For: 38   Against: 33

5. Sam Cowan: 1946/47
Lasted: 30 games
Won: 20   Drew: 6   Lost: 4   For: 53   Against: 27

BERMUDA SHORTS

The beautiful British colonial island of Bermuda has a strong link with City, thanks entirely to the Blues' Bermudian striker Shaun Goater. 'The Goat' was even honoured with his own tribute day – 21 June 2001 – officially named 'Shaun Goater Day'. Thousands turned out to watch his motorcade drive through the capital's streets. It's not an annual event, but is now famous in its own right and perhaps should be a yearly occurrence – imagine the City fans who would flock over to pay homage to The Goat!

BANANAS!

The arrival of the inflatable yellow perils, mainly prevalent in the 1988/89 season, were a colourful affair, especially on the Kippax or at away grounds and the Blues' faithful were rightly praised by the media for bringing some much-needed humour back to a dull period for the club and football in general. Why bananas? Well, one theory is the club have been known to slip-up on a few banana skins in the past, so that's in with a shout. Another is that Imre Varadi, a crowd favourite of the day, had a surname that sounded a *bit* like 'banana'. Frank Newton, a City fan and computer analyst, is considered the Fyffesfather, however, as he is credited as the man who introduced the first 'nana to Maine Road after borrowing it from a mate in Leeds back in 1987. The craze of bringing various blow-up bits of fruit, toys, monsters and suchlike caught on and supporters at other clubs had their own varied themes, one of the best being Stoke City and their legions of Pink Panthers, Grimsby Town and their 'Harry the Haddocks' and Norwich City with their yellow canaries. They made something of a minor comeback in 2006/07 and will always be welcome where the Blues are playing.

PROJECT BLUE BOOK

There have been several books of note on the Blues that are worthy of mention. Andrew Ward and Ray Goble produced *Manchester City: A Complete Record* (Breedon Books, 1987) and updated it in 1993 – an indispensable work for anyone writing about the Blues and a completely new version was released in 2006 by Gary James. In 1990 James and Steve Cawley released *The Pride of Manchester*

(Polar). Alec Johnson's *The Battle for Manchester City* (Mainstream, 1994) charts the bitter takeover by Francis Lee. Gary James was also responsible for the excellent *Football with a Smile: The Authorised Biography of Joe Mercer* (Polar, 1993) and the equally impressive *Manchester – The Greatest City* (Polar, 1998).

Among the earlier written works were Mike Doyle's *Manchester City – My Team* (Souvenir Press, 1977), and John Harding's *Billy Meredith* (Breedon Books, 1985). Mark Hodkinson's superb *Blue Moon* (Mainstream, 1999) is a must-read and there have been several other works plus a couple on former City players: *Priceless* by Rodney Marsh (Headline, 2001) and *Bowles* by Steve Bidmead (Virgin, 2002). More recent titles include *Kinkladze: The Perfect 10* by some chancer from Manchester, *Lows, Highs and Balti Pies* by Steve Mingle, *Farewell to Maine Road* by Gary James, *Reluctant Hero* by Colin Bell and *Feed the Goat* by Shaun Goater. *Bobby Johnstone – The Passing of an Age* by John Leigh was the first major City book of 2007. In more recent years there have been tomes such as *The Joe Corrigan Story* (by yours truly and Big Joe), *Trautmann's Journey: From Hitler Youth to FA Cup Legend* by Catrine Clay and in 2011 autobiographies of two City legends were released with former captains Paul Lake and Andy Morrison both sharing their life stories with the masses.

THE BOYS IN BLUE

City released the classic 'The Boys in Blue' in 1972 to an unsuspecting (judging by sales) record-buying public. The song, on the RCA label, was penned by none other than Kevin Godley and Lol Creme – half of the hugely successful 1970s Mancunian band 10cc, and was definitely one of the better football tunes of the time. Though it failed to chart, it became the anthem of Saturday afternoons spent at Maine Road for over 20 years. The much-loved tune is still played every now and then, and got an emotional airing for the final game at Maine Road in April 2003.

CARETAKER MANAGERS

Over Man City's history so far, nine men have taken on the role of caretaker boss – here are the men who steadied the ship as best they could . . .

Albert Alexander Snr 1925–6
31 matches in charge

| Pld: 31 | W: 13 | D: 8 | L: 10 | F: 80 | A: 56 |

Wilf Wild 1947
16 matches in charge

| Pld: 16 | W: 5 | D: 5 | L: 6 | F: 20 | A: 18 |

Johnny Hart 1965
5 matches in charge

| P: 5 | W: 1 | D: 3 | L: 1 | F: 4 | A: 5 |

Tony Book 1973 (7 matches), 1980 (1 match), 1989 (3 matches), 1993 (1 match)
12 matches in charge

| P: 12 | W: 2 | D: 4 | L: 6 | F: 12 | A: 14 |

Asa Hartford 1996
8 matches in charge

| Pld: 8 | W: 3 | D: 0 | L: 5 | F: 8 | A: 13 |

Phil Neal 1996
10 matches in charge

| Pld: 10 | W: 2 | D: 1 | L: 7 | F: 11 | A: 19 |

Stuart Pearce 2005
9 matches in charge

| Pld: 9 | W: 4 | D: 4 | L: 1 | F: 13 | A: 7 |

Committee managed 1912
2 matches

| Pld: 2 | W: 2 | D: 0 | L:0 | F: 2 | A: 0 |

Unknown caretaker 1946 (between Wilf Wild and Sam Cowan)
3 matches

| Pld: 3 | W: 2 | D: 1 | L: 0 | F: 3 | A: 1 |

HEY, BRO!

There have been sets of 24 brothers who have represented City at one level or another, including trialists. The first pair to play for City in the same match were Albert and Peter Fairclough, who signed from Eccles Borough on the same day in 1913. George Dorsett played for the club for six years before his brother Joe arrived at Maine Road in 1910. Futcher twins Paul and Ron, joined the Blues from Luton in 1978, while Manchester lads Dave and Gary Bennett represented the Blues at most levels and Darren and Jason Beckford worked their way through the ranks and into the first team, though neither ever gained a sustained run. Peter Barnes' brother Mike was on the club's books for a couple of years and both Paul Lake's brothers, Mike and Dave, were on trial with City in 1985 and 1988 respectively. There was also Ian and David Brightwell, Jeff and Jim Whitley, Nick and Anthony Fenton and, of late, Shaun and Bradley Wright-Phillips and the D'Laryea twins with Kolo and Yaya Touré the latest siblings to represent the Blues.

The full list is:

Barnes	Peter and Mike*
Beckford	Darren and Jason
Bennett	Dave and Gary*
Brightwell	Ian and David
Broad	Jimmy and Tommy
Caton	Tommy and Paul*
Cookson	Jimmy and Sammy
Corbett	Frank and Vic
Cunliffe	Bobby and David
Dorsett	George and Joe
D'Laryea	Jon and Nathan*
Etuhu	Kelvin and Dickson
Fairclough	Albert and Peter
Fenton	Nick and Anthony*
Futcher	Paul and Ron
Hynds	Tom and John
Lake	Paul, Mike* and Dave*
Logan	Carlos* and Shaleum
Moffatt	Robert and James
Ross	Frank and George
Skogsrud	Tom* and Kim*
Touré	Kolo and Yaya
Whitley	Jeff and Jim
Wright-Phillips	Shaun and Bradley

* Never played for the first team

AYE, AYE, SKIPPER

The Blues can list some of football's true greats as their former skippers. Billy Meredith was the first captain to lift the FA Cup after a 1–0 win over Bolton Wanderers in 1904. Sam Cowan captained City to no less than three FA Cup finals and Sam Barkas led the Blues to the 1946/47 Second Division title. Roy Paul's grit and determination to drive his side to success was evident as City returned to pick up the FA Cup in 1956 after being beaten at the same stage a year earlier. Paul had vowed to take his team back and win the trophy just as Sam Cowan had done 22 years earlier, and was as good as his word, threatening his team-mates that they'd have him to deal with if his prophecy was derailed.

City's most successful captain was Tony Book. The influential, no-nonsense full-back was inspirational as City won 5 trophies in 4 years, including every domestic honour plus the European Cup Winners' Cup. Keith Curle was a great leader and wore the armband when the Blues achieved their highest finishes in Division One for 14 years – fifth – for two successive campaigns in 1991 and 1992. Mike Doyle was the last captain to lift silverware in 1976 after beating Newcastle 2–1 in the League Cup final and Andy Morrison led the Blues 'kicking and screaming' out of Division Two in 1999. Stuart Pearce's one season as skipper saw the side break many records and win the Second Division Championship in great style under his impeccable leadership. Ali Benarbia became a member of an exclusive band of foreign players to skipper City after taking the armband for the 2002/03 season. Others include Bermudian striker Shaun Goater and Dutchman Gerard Wiekens, while Richard Dunne replaced Sylvain Distin as skipper in 2005. Inspirational Argentinian striker Carlos Tevez took the armband from Kolo Touré for the 2010/11 season – one of City's best modern-day seasons, with City winning the FA Cup and claiming a place in the Champions League for the first time.

TOP PLAYERS LIST

In 2006, the official Manchester City magazine conducted a survey of favourite players, inviting supporters to name their top three all-time City stars. Here's the Top 25:

1. Colin Bell
2. Georgiou Kinkladze
3. Francis Lee
4. Joe Corrigan
5. Shaun Wright-Phillips
6. Shaun Goater
7. Mike Summerbee
8. Dennis Tueart
9. Niall Quinn
10. Dave Watson
11. Mike Doyle
12. Bert Trautmann
13. David White
14. Uwe Rosler
15. Peter Barnes
16. Rodney Marsh
17. Paul Lake
18. Ali Benarbia
19. Sylvain Distin
20. Alan Oakes
21. Neil Young
22. Asa Hartford
23. Frank Swift
24. Tony Book
25. Joey Barton

CELEBRATIONS

Andy Hinchcliffe's five-fingered salute to the Manchester United fans housed in the Platt Lane End after his header made the score 5–1 to the Blues in September 1989 is a perfect example of how to celebrate a goal. Nick Weaver's 'catch-me-if-you-can' celebratory dash after saving a decisive penalty in the 1999 play-off final against Gillingham will live long in the memory and it was only Andy Morrison wrestling him to the ground that stopped him from continuing his run across London. Paul Dickov's last-gasp equaliser in the same game will take some beating, too.

Darren Huckerby scored against Millwall at the New Den in 2001 but due to a history of violent clashes between Millwall and City fans, both clubs took the decision to ban away fans for each match between the two teams during the 2001/02 season. When Huckerby scored at the end where several thousand City fans should have been housed, he ran to the empty stand and applauded with his hands over his head regardless and was joined by Shaun Goater and Shaun Wright-Phillips as the players sent a message to missing army. Bernardo Corradi knighted Joey Barton with a corner flag after notching the first of his two goals against Fulham in 2006 and Georgios Samaras tended to celebrate by mysteriously pointing to the sky. In 2009, Carlos Tevez introduced the backside wiggle, apparently inspired by a dance his brother does, when celebrating goals for the Blues.

BADGE OF HOUNOUR

City's current club crest was first adopted in 1997, a result of the previous crest being ineligible for registration as a trademark. The badge is based on the coat of arms of the City of Manchester, and consists of a shield in front of a golden eagle. The shield features a ship on its upper half representing the Manchester Ship Canal, and three diagonal stripes in the lower half, for the city's three rivers. The bottom of the badge bears the Latin motto *Superbia in Proelio*, which translates as Pride in Battle. Above the eagle and shield are three stars. City have previously worn two other crests on their shirts. The first, introduced in 1970, was based on designs which had been used on official club documentation since the mid-1960s. It consisted of a round badge which used the same shield as the current crest, inside a circle bearing the name of the club. In 1972 this was replaced by a variation which replaced the lower half of the shield with the red rose of Lancashire. On occasions when the Blues played in a major cup final, the usual crest was not used and instead shirts bearing a badge of the arms of the City of Manchester are used, as a symbol of pride in representing the city at a major event. This practice originates from a time when the players' shirts did not normally bear a badge of any kind, but has continued throughout the history of the club.

BLUE MOONIES

City's official mascot is Moonchester, an inhabitant of, where else, the Blue Moon. The combination of his home and his love for Manchester City has developed into the name of Moon (Blue Moon) chester (Manchester City), hence the name Moonchester. It's simple, really. Moonchester was unveiled on 16 August 1996 before the Manchester City v Ipswich Town game at Maine Road. This was the first ever Premier League game to be shown on Sky on a Friday night. City won 1–0 thanks to a 25th-minute Steve Lomas goal.

Moonbeam is Moonchester's girlfriend and she made her debut on Boxing Day 2001 after Moonchester put out an appeal through the Jodrell Bank telescope to find a partner. It's all true and there is documentation to prove as much.

RHYTHM & BLUES

Oasis are probably the most famous City followers and the Gallagher brothers, Noel and Liam, were regulars at Maine Road before their careers really took off. Mike Pickering of M People, Billy Duffy from The Cult and iconic guitarist Johnny Marr, formerly of The Smiths and Electronic, are all lifelong supporters as are the entire ensemble of Doves.

Damon Gough, better known as Badly Drawn Boy, Rick Wakeman and Take That member Jason Orange are also City fans. Another boy-band member, Max from The Wanted, is a big Blue as is vocalist Adio from Kid British. Ex-Smith Mike Joyce is a die-hard, Rob Gretton, former manager of New Order and part-owner of the Hacienda, was a loyal Blue and season-ticket holder until his untimely death several years ago, as well as two of Manchester's most influential songwriters, the late Ian Curtis of Joy Division and Mark E. Smith of The Fall. Oh, and we mustn't forget Reni from The Stone Roses and Gilly from The Inspiral Carpets.

SPORTING CELEBRITY BLUES

World champion boxer Ricky Hatton is a lifelong City fan as is fellow boxer Michael Gomez. Olympic swimmer James Hickman, England rugby union stars Will Greenwood and

Andy Farrell, plus rugby league star Shaun Edwards and cricket legends Andrew Flintoff and Phil DeFreitas are all Blues fans.

CELEBRITY FANS – TV & FILM

Television presenter John Stapleton, roly-poly comedians Eddie Large and the late Bernard Manning have all followed the club since their childhood days, and Large was even a regular on the City bench for a time during the 1980s. Marsha Thomason, co-star of Disney movie *The Haunted Mansion* and former James Bond star Timothy Dalton also support the Blues, as do soap stars Jeff Hordley, Bruce Jones, Sally Lyndsay and Amanda Barrie. Archie Kelly from *Phoenix Nights*, comedian Jason Manford and David Threlfall – Frank Gallagher of Channel 4's *Shameless* – are Blues. Craig Cash from BBC's *The Royle Family* and actor Warren Clarke support City, too.

CENTENARY

Ardwick FC had suffered one devastating blow after another and in March 1894 the club was on the verge of extinction. Three crushing defeats – 5–0 at Notts County, 10–2 at Small Heath and 6–0 at Lincoln City – crippling financial problems and a massive turnover of players meant that it would be extremely unlikely that Ardwick FC would return for another season. Ardwick secretary Joshua Parlby had the foresight to form a new club from the ashes of Ardwick and effectively began from scratch. On 21 April 1894 – a week after Ardwick had finished last but one of

14 sides in Division Two, it was announced in the *Manchester Evening Mail* that a new company, namely Manchester City Football Club, was to be formed for the start of the 1894/95 season. On 1 September Manchester City lost 4–2 at Bury and earned their first point two days later against Burton Albion. The Blues had been officially born and were on their way. The club 'celebrated' its centenary in 1994 with a 3–0 defeat at Chelsea on 31 August – almost 100 years exactly since the first match. Let's hope the next hundred years are happier!

10 MOST DRAMATIC LAST GAMES OF THE SEASON

Over the years the Blues have had a reputation for providing the fans with end-of-season drama. Here are 10 games that had supporters on the edge of their seats until the last kick of the match, complete with the pre-match scenario and end result . . .

1.   **30 May 1999 v Gillingham**
      Result needed: A win to secure promotion
      Actual result: Won on penalties

2.   **11 May 1968 v Newcastle**
      Result needed: A win to win the league title
      Actual result: Won 4–3

3.   **7 May 2000 v Blackburn Rovers**
      Result needed: A draw to secure promotion
      Actual result: Won 4–1

4.   **11 May 1985 v Charlton Athletic**
       Result needed: A win to secure promotion
       Actual result: Won 5–1

5.   **14 May 1983 v Luton Town**
       Result needed: A draw to avoid relegation
       Actual result: Lost 1–0 and were relegated

6.   **13 May 1989 Bradford City**
       Result needed: A point to secure promotion
       Actual result: A 1–1 draw!

7.   **5 May 1996 v Liverpool**
       Result needed: A win to have a chance of survival
       Actual result: A 2–2 draw

8.   **15 May 2005 v Middlesbrough**
       Result needed: A win to secure a UEFA Cup spot
       Actual result: Drew 1–1

9.   **27 April 1974 v Man Utd**
       Result needed: Win to confirm United's relegation
       Actual result: Won 1–0

10.   **3 May 1998 v Stoke City**
       Result needed: Win for a chance of avoiding relegation
       Actual result: Won 5–2 and were relegated anyway

STIFFS

City's reserve side had been in existence since 1892/93 when Ardwick FC first formed a second eleven for their burgeoning squad. Ardwick's transformation into Manchester City didn't alter the reserve set-up and for nineteen years the Blues' second string played in the Lancashire Combination, winning twice and finishing runners-up twice. The Central League was formed in 1911/12, encompassing a larger and more geographically spread pool of reserve sides. Amazingly, it would take 67 years for City to win the Central League when reserve boss Dave Ewing and team captain Ged Keegan successfully guided the side to the title – finally.

They were relegated for the first time in 1981/82 to the newly-formed Central League Division Two. The club's second reserve championship was in 1986/87, which was also, bizarrely, the same year the senior squad was relegated from Division One. The team consisted largely of the exceptional 1986 FA Youth Cup-winning squad and augured well for the club's future. Following sweeping changes to the reserve league set-up in time for the 1999/2000 season, the Blues, coached by Asa Hartford, were put into the top division and duly won the title by seven clear points. City's reward was promotion to the Barclays Premiership Reserve League – the highest level a second eleven can play at. In 2010/11, the reserves became officially rebranded as the Elite Development Squad (EDS).

CENTURIONS

The Blues have clocked up 100 goals or more in the league on five occasions. The record is 108 set in 1926/27 when finishing third in Division Two and the figure was equalled for the 2001/02 season, with Stuart Pearce missing a last-minute penalty in the final game and blowing the chance of setting a new record and completing his own personal century of career goals at club level. In 1927/28 City again reached three figures for a second successive season and this time they won the Division Two Championship. There were 107 strikes during the Division One title-winning season of 1936/37 and in 1957/58 the Blues scored 104 and conceded 100 to finish fifth in the top division! It's never been done before or since.

MEN AT THE TOP

Of all the chairmen Manchester City have had, nobody made more of an impression than Peter J. Swales. A true Blue in every sense of the word, Swales, promoted to the chair in October 1973, tried everything within his power to re-establish City as a major force in England after the halcyon Mercer–Allison days of the late 1960s. Within his first year at the helm he had sacked Ron Saunders, appointed Tony Book, seen City lose a League Cup final and watched Law backheel United into Division Two.

When Francis Lee entered the frame and showed a genuine interest in becoming chairman, Swales's grip on the club finally began to weaken. The bitter battle for Manchester City had begun and in 1994 fan-power finally forced Peter Swales out of Maine Road. In 1998, financial director David Bernstein became chairman and he oversaw the Blues' return from Division Two to the Premiership in successive seasons before chairman John Wardle took the helm in 2001. In 2008, Abu Dhabi-based tycoon Sheikh Mansour bought City from former Thai Prime Minister Thaksin Shinawatra and employed Khaldoon al-Mubarak as the new chairman – the club hasn't looked back since.

CHAMPIONS!

City have twice been crowned champions of England but in typical City style, they had to wait until the last day of the season on each occasion. The historic first was in 1936/37 when an Eric Brook-inspired City beat Sheffield Wednesday 4–1 to clinch the trophy. In 1967/68 City travelled to Newcastle United, needing a win to ensure Manchester United and Liverpool could not overtake them on the final day. City won 4–3 and United had to settle for runners-up spot.

City have won seven Division Two titles. The first was in 1898/99 and then four years later in 1902/03 and again in 1909/10 – the latter two following relegation the previous season. In 1927/28 City pipped Leeds United to the title by two points and in 1946/47 the Blues won the League by four points over Burnley and enjoyed a 22-match unbeaten run along the way. The 1965/66 title was a prelude to the silverware-laden days of Mercer and Allison, and Kevin Keegan's entertainers were crowned the 'new' Division One Champions in great style, ten points clear of West Bromwich Albion in 2001/02.

NO PLACE LIKE HOME

The City of Manchester Stadium became City's new home from the start of the 2003/04 season following 80 years at Maine Road and is widely regarded as one of the best grounds in Britain and Europe. With a capacity of 48,000, the futuristic design was initially home to the hugely successful 2002 Commonwealth Games held in the city. It's already hosted several major pop concerts, including Oasis, Red Hot Chili Peppers and Take That and England played two friendlies at Eastlands against Iceland and Japan. In 2008, it hosted the UEFA Cup final between Rangers and Zenit St Petersburg.

BLUE CHRISTMASES

City have played no less than 44 Christmas Day matches through the years. When the players should have been opening presents and carving the turkey, they were representing the club in cold and frosty grounds up and down the country for what was then a pittance. The last time the Blues played on Christmas Day was half a century ago in 1957, when they lost 2–1 at Burnley in front of 28,000 shivering fans.

The complete record is:
Pld: 44   W: 14   D: 11   L: 19   F: 74   A: 86

NONE SHALL PASS

With 26 clean sheets in all competitions, Nicky Weaver held the record for stop-outs achieved during the 1998/99 season. He kept a further 19 in all competitions the following season and both times City won promotion, underlining his value to the side. However, in 2010/11, Joe Hart broke that record, having kept 27 clean sheets, the last of which was in the FA Cup final victory over Stoke.

THESE COLOURS DON'T RUN

Gorton FC are believed to have worn black shirts with a large white cross on the front, though it is difficult to be 100 per cent accurate as few records remain from so long ago. Ardwick have been described as wearing mainly white but it was when Manchester City were first formed that the colour blue is first mentioned – and Cambridge Blue at that – plus grey shorts. The shorts were ditched in 1896/97 in favour of white shorts with a plum-coloured change strip.

The favourite and what are believed to be the traditional colours of City – the light blue shirts – didn't arrive until some years later. There have been numerous change strips in the past and most of them have been since the 1980s when a garish selection of colours and designs were selected for the club's away kit.

The red and black striped shirt from the late 1960s is a firm favourite with fans and is still used as a third-choice kit today. Many consider the luminous yellow and black striped strip from the 1998 Division Two play-off final also to be lucky. The City players now wear laser blue for the home strip and have done since 1997/98. The 2002/03 away kit was a retro design from the mid-1970s – white with a black-and-red slash across the front. Suppliers of the kit have been Umbro, Kappa, Le Coq Sportif and Reebok. Umbro returned to make City's kit in 2008 and remained the suppliers going into the 2011/12 campaign.

BRIEF ENCOUNTER

Steve Coppell's 30-day stay as manager of Manchester City in 1996 remains a record for its brevity. An embarrassment to all concerned, Coppell walked out of the club, ashen-faced within a month but proved himself to be a top coach and manager elsewhere in later years, particularly at Reading. Maybe he just wanted the record as the shortest reign for a City boss! For the record, his league stats as manager are:

Pld: 6   W: 2   D: 1   L: 3   F: 7   A: 10

WE DON'T LIKE CRICKET

Two former City players who were also first-class cricketers were 'Patsy' Hendren and Jack Dyson. Hendren played 51 Test matches for England and scored over 40,000 runs for Middlesex. The well-built winger played only twice for the Blues during the 1908/09 season. Jack Dyson was a talented all-rounder for Lancashire scoring 4,433 runs and taking 161 wickets between 1954 and 1964. As one sporting season ended, the other began so holidays were a thing of fancy until his retirement from at least one of the sports. He played 72 games for City (1951–61) in all competitions and scored 29 goals, including one in the 1956 FA Cup final. The irrepressible forward also broke his leg twice during the 1957/58 season.

OFF TO A FLYER

Every footballer dreams of a debut where everything turns out the way they imagined, whether it be a hat-trick, a match-saving tackle or a wondrous last-minute penalty save – depending on the position the debutant plays in, of course. Few experience such a dream start to their careers but there have been some notable exceptions. Fred Howard scored all four goals in a 4–1 win over Liverpool in January 1913 and then scored a goal in each of the next two league matches. He then went seven without a goal before adding five in the last six games of the season. He also scored three more against Liverpool the next season and then a single goal in each of the next three encounters, making it an amazing ten in six games – the Merseyside Reds must have been sick of the sight of him!

Jimmy Constantine hit a debut treble against Millwall in 1946, though he had previously played for the club during the Second World War, hitting 25 in 34 in the Football League North and FA Cup. Paulo Wanchope enjoyed a memorable home debut against Sunderland in August 2000 when he struck three of the goals in a 4–2 victory, though he had played for City away from home and failed to score prior to that. Many players have managed a goal on their first appearance for City and Niall Quinn is among them. His towering header against Chelsea in March 1990, earning the Blues a valuable 1–1 draw, was the start of many important goals the Irishman scored for the club. Mikhail Kavelashvili scored against Manchester United on his debut in 1996, but ended up on the losing side in a 3–2 defeat. Robinho announced his arrival in Manchester by scoring with a free-kick against Chelsea barely 15 minutes into his City career.

At the other end of the scale, Carlo Nash endured a nightmarish beginning to his career at Maine Road after being forced to pick the ball out of the net four times in the first 35 minutes against a rampant Arsenal in April 2001, though none were his fault and things improved considerably from then on. Bernardo Corradi joined a select club of reluctant members when he was shown the red card on his City debut at Chelsea in 2006.

ONE HELL OF A BEATING

The Blues have handed out – and been on the end of – a few thrashings over the years. Briefly, the worst of the worst are as follows:

1894	Division One	Small Heath 10–2 City
1896	FA Cup first round	Preston 6–0 City
1906	Division One	Everton 9–1 City
1962	League Cup fifth round	Birmingham 6–0 City

BEST DEFENCE

City conceded just 29 goals in 34 games during the 1902/03 campaign, though the 33 conceded in 46 Division Two games in 1998/99 read even better on a games-to-goals basis. The worst season for the Blues' defence was in 1962/63 when 102 goals were leaked and, hardly surprisingly, City were relegated.

DERBIES

There was a time when City dominated the Manchester derby, but it's a long time since the Blues completed a league double over their cross-city rivals. Favourite derby days include the 4–1 away win for City with Franny Lee notching a hat-trick and, in particular, the 1–0 win at Old Trafford in 1974 which rubber-stamped United's relegation to Division Two. The 1989 massacre at Maine Road, where the Blues romped home 5–1, remains among the Blues' fans favourite games of all time, while the 4–1 and 3–1 victories at the City of Manchester Stadium restored Blue pride in the last few years.

Regrets – we've had a few! Somehow a 2–0 half-time lead became 2–3 by full-time in November 1993, but that's enough about losing to the Rags.

Though not as glamorous, derby days with Oldham Athletic, Stockport County, Bury and even Macclesfield Town have all caused a few headaches, with Oldham and Stockport in particular excelling in the Maine Road fixtures. Bolton Wanderers are a derby of sorts. Save for Bolton, most of these, with respect, are minor derbies and likely to be consigned to the history books following City's recent renaissance – hopefully! The 2011 FA Cup semi-final at Wembley was arguably the highest-profile Manchester derby of all-time.

CAN YOU SEE US ON THE BOX?

In 1979 the Blues were the subject of a one-hour documentary simply called *City* and shown by ITV; a fascinating behind-the-scenes look at the Peter Swales and Malcolm Allison relationship with some unforgettable moments between the two. Cataloguing a poor season, the problems that ran to the core of the club were there for all to see in a genuine warts-and-all programme. It culminated with the return of Allison as Crystal Palace coach in an FA Cup match at Maine Road. It was never repeated and today gathers dust in the television archives of Granada.

BBC1's flagship evening magazine *Nationwide* (a portent of the misery to come?), featuring Sue Lawley, made for riveting viewing for City fans as the programme covered the Blues' 1978 Division One campaign. Once again, cameras were granted access to wherever they wished and though each segment was rarely more than five minutes long, it was national exposure for the club and an extra bonus for the supporters. In 2006, Channel M launched a weekly magazine show dedicated to the Blues entitled *Inside MCFC* and at the end of the 2009/10 season, Endemol commissioned *Blue Moon Rising*, a documentary of a year in the life of the club through the eyes of a group of supporters and their faithful people carrier, Helios.

ALAN ATTACK!

When City played FC Salzburg at home in late 2010, a substitute appeared with the name 'Alan' on his back. The amused City fans adopted Alan immediately and began singing his name and cheering his every touch. He later sent a special Christmas message to the Blues' faithful after receiving fan mail and numerous requests for an interview.

NIL BY (GOAL) MOUTH

City created a piece of unwanted history when they went 7 consecutive Premiership home games without scoring in 2006/07. It meant that City had only managed to score in 7 of their home games all season, 12 ending without a goal for the home side and earning the Blues the nickname 'Manchester City nil' within media circles. In a generally poor season for scoring all round, it was the lowest goals tally the club has ever had with the top scorer, Joey Barton, ending with a paltry 6. On the flipside, the 14 clean sheets City kept during 2006/07 was (at the time) the club's highest tally in the Premiership.

THE POZNAN

When Lech Poznan visited the City of Manchester Stadium for their Europa League clash in 2010, the 3,000 Polish fans turned their back on the pitch during the match and began jumping up and down in unison. The City fans then began doing 'The Poznan' as the season progressed, reaching the stage when up to 30,000 were doing it at the same time during a 5–0 win over Sunderland in April 2011. Perhaps the best Poznans of all were saved for the FA Cup semi-final against Man Utd and the final against Stoke when the fans celebrated in style and caught the imagination of the football world.

THE SECOND WORLD WAR YEARS

It was a time of change as City began the 1938/39 season. It was Wilf Wild's seventh year in charge and the shock of being relegated as reigning champions was still sinking in. City began the campaign with more or less the same squad and when a 5–0 win over Swansea was followed by a 3–0 victory over Chesterfield, there seemed little need to bring in new faces.

The next four games, however, – all defeats – suggested otherwise. The 6–1 home loss to Millwall convinced Wild that a potent forward line was not enough to take the Blues back up to Division One and he began to reshape his defence. Bert Sproston and Eric Westwood were signed as full-backs and their influence immediately inspired City to win 5 consecutive games in November. The goals were still flying in and 9–3, 5–2 and 5–1 were recorded over four days at Christmas.

City were still off the pace of the leaders and despite an unbeaten run of 10 games on the run-in, they finished in a hugely disappointing sixth position. Only six players had managed to appear more than 30 times in an unsettling time for the club, and the rest of Britain.

Just three games into the 1939/40 season and the Second World War began. The Football League programme was abandoned and a Western Regional League was set up. Many City players were called-up for armed service duty, as football became no more than a welcome distraction.

Games took little more importance than friendlies and though gates would occasionally top 60,000, the majority of matches were witnessed by fewer than 10,000. Wilf Wild remained manager throughout the war and when Britain and the allies finally defeated Hitler, the Football League reformed.

With the nation still celebrating the victory and return of loved ones, Wilf Wild prepared City for the 1946/47 season. It would be his last in charge as the Blues paved the way for the return of a favourite son, Sam Cowan.

WAY BACK WHEN

This is what was happening in the world when Maine Road opened its doors for the first time in August 1923:

3 March   The first issue of *Time* magazine was published.

28 April   The inaugural FA Cup final – known as the White Horse Final – was played at Wembley Stadium. Bolton Wanderers beat West Ham 2–0. Liverpool were crowned champions with Sunderland runners-up.

1 September A devastating earthquake killed more than 200,000 people in Tokyo and Yokohama, Japan. The quake measured 8.3 on the Richter scale.

3 November Cecil B. DeMille's biblical epic *The Ten Commandments* was premiered at picture houses around the world. It cost $1.5million to make. Other movies released around this time included *The Hunchback of Notre Dame*, starring Lon Chaney, while Harold Lloyd released the classic *Safety Last*.

26 November The BBC made its first experimental transatlantic radio broadcast to the USA.

FOUR-LEGGED FRIENDS

Every dog has their day, so they say, but one hapless pooch found its way tragically into club history on the day after Guy Fawkes' Night in 1920, when the Main Stand at City's Hyde Road ground burned to the ground. With it went all of the club's records, but worse still, City's faithful hound, Nell, also perished in the flames. The cause was not, as first suspected, a firework, but a stray cigarette butt. Perhaps the whole sorry episode is the reason why the Blues resisted selling hot dogs at the ground until recently.

Several Moss Side strays have enjoyed a moment of fame by doing a lap of the Maine Road pitch and evading stewards with a burst of pace that would inevitably have the Kippax roaring for the current manager to 'sign him up!' One cheeky mutt, possibly leaning towards the red side of Manchester, once ran up to the goal posts at the Platt Lane end and promptly cocked his leg up. Barefaced cheek! There was also the comical sight of Yugoslavian City defender Dragoslav Stepanovic chasing one mutt around the pitch after an impromptu pitch invasion in 1979.

Clive Allen named his dog Nella, which spelled backwards, of course, reads 'Allen'. Former City skipper Sylvain Distin is the proud owner of a pet Labrador.

BLUE IS THE COLOUR?

There is evidence that the club have worn blue since 1892 or earlier. West Gorton (St Marks) originally played in scarlet and black, and reports dating from 1884 describe the team wearing black jerseys bearing a white cross, showing the club's origins as a church side – it might also be the origins of why many City fans say 'Oh my God!' so often during matches. Famously, the idea to have red and black striped shirts for away colours came from legendary coach Malcom Allison, who believed that adopting the colours of AC Milan would inspire City to glory.

LEGEND: NEIL YOUNG

1959 to 1972
Appearances: 409 + 3 as a substitute
Goals: 108
Position: Forward
Born: Fallowfield, Manchester

Neil Young played a number of key roles in the City forward line before Joe Mercer gave him the no. 10 shirt for keeps and then contentedly sat back as the Manchester-born striker began to fulfil his considerable potential. Young possessed a cultured left foot and was at the heart of the Blues' halcyon days when the club swept away all in its path. In fact, it could be argued that Young had a more substantial role than anyone else during the glory days, having scored crucial goals at times when important matches were finely balanced.

For instance, it was his left-foot cracker that won the 1969 FA Cup final against Leicester City and Young was, without doubt, a major influence in City's European Cup Winners' Cup triumph a year later after scoring and then winning a penalty in the 2–1 win over Gornik Zabrze. He was also the top scorer when the Blues last lifted the Division One Championship trophy with 19 and bagged a couple in the final and deciding game at Newcastle United. He signed for Preston in January 1972 for £48,000 after 13 years at Maine Road. Recently honoured in a series of testimonial events organised mainly by supporters, Young was mystifyingly overlooked at international level, but his place with the heroes of yesteryear is guaranteed among all Blues followers. Sadly, Youngy died early in 2011, but not before the City fans had held a special tribute away to Leicester City, all wearing red and black scarves and dancing 'The Poznan' in the 24th minute of the game – the same time he scored the winner against the same club back in 1969.

QUICK ON THE DRAW

In 1993/94, the Blues drew 18 matches (11 scoring and 7 no-score draws), a club record. With City failing to score in another nine league games that season, it was hardly surprising that the top scorer, Mike Sheron, had only six goals. The fewest drawn games in a season was exactly a hundred years earlier when only two of 28 league games ended with honours being even. Three ties from 42 games played in 1959/60 is an even more impressive – or unimpressive, depending on how you view it – figure. The highest-scoring draws were against Everton in 1925/26 and Chelsea in 1936/37 when both games ended 4–4. There was a 6–6 draw during the Second World War, against Stockport County (1939), but the record does not stand officially.

ILL EAGLE?

'Eddie the Eagle', the plastic suspended bird that dangled from the new Kippax Stand roof towards the end of the Blues' tenure at Maine Road, was placed there to prevent pigeons nesting and subsequently pooping on the punters below. The unofficial mascot didn't follow the Blues to the City of Manchester Stadium in 2003, however, and packs of cocky doves have been sighted during certain games – bring Eddie back!

WHEN CHAMPIONS WERE CHAMPIONS

City have ventured into the competition of European Champions – when it was strictly for winners of the respective European leagues and not like today, when every man and his dog can qualify – just once. The Blues went out at the first hurdle. Naivety liberally mixed with inexperience no doubt played a large part of the Blues' swift exit, but Malcolm Allison's statement that his team would 'terrify Europe' didn't seem to help much, it has to be said. Reigning champions City began the 1968/69 season full of hope and expectations were high. Little was known about Turkish Champions Fenerbahce when they ran out at Maine Road for the opening round's first leg. The hugely experienced visitors proved to be master defensive tacticians and held the Blues to a frustrating 0–0 draw. The second leg, played in front of a 45,000-strong hostile Turkish crowd, looked to be tilting City's way when Tony Coleman scored the opening goal, but the home side bided their time, continually applied pressure and eventually won 2–1. A tough lesson had been learned, but City would put it to good use just 12 months later.

POLE DANCING

The European Cup Winners' Cup is a now-defunct trophy that once pitted the domestic cup winners from all over Europe in one competition – until the UEFA bureaucrats decided on making the European Cup into a cash-making monster and tinker with the UEFA Cup to the point it's only really for Champions League failures: madness. The ECWC was a tournament that Manchester City took to immediately, winning it at the first attempt and almost successfully defending it. The FA Cup final victory over Leicester City in 1969 had given Joe Mercer's side a fast-track back into Europe following the European Cup disappointment 12 months earlier. In what would prove to be an exciting adventure on the continent, the Blues began their journey with a terrific display of gutsy, attacking football to hold Atletico Bilbao to a 3–3 draw in Spain and then dispatched them confidently 3–0 at Maine Road. Belgian side SK Lierse were soundly beaten 3–0 on their own soil and then 5–0 in Manchester.

Next up were Portuguese outfit Academica Coimbra. They proved a much tougher nut to crack, but it was the Blues' turn to play spoilers with a 0–0 draw in Portugal followed

THE MAN CITY MISCELLANY

by a hard-fought 1–0 home win, Tony Towers scoring the vital winner with a penalty shoot-out just seconds away – the lessons of European Cup failure were being put to good use. City moved into the semi-finals to face German side Schalke 04, losing the away leg 1–0, but, in one of the best performances by a Joe Mercer side, City ran riot at Maine Road winning 5–1 and so progressed to the final. At last, Allison's prediction that City would be the *enfant terrible* of European football became reality, only one year late.

Around 6,000 City fans then made the midweek trek to Vienna to see a deserved 2–1 win over crack Polish side Gornik Zabrze, with the goals coming from a Franny Lee penalty conversion and Neil Young. The conditions were atrocious and in weather more typical of Manchester than Vienna, torrential rain lashed down on the uncovered crowd throughout the game. Never mind, City had their first – and to date only – European trophy. Many clubs, having said that, are still waiting for such an honour.

The Blues began the defence of their trophy in 1970 with a narrow win over Northern Irish side Linfield. A 1–0 home win was nearly not enough as the plucky minnows beat City 2–1 in Belfast. Only Franny Lee's strike enabled the defending champions to limp through on the away goals rule. A more professional display against Honved resulted in a 3–0 aggregate win after victories at home and away, setting up a rematch against Gornik Zabrze.

An awesome crowd of 100,000 buoyed the Polish side to a 2–0 first leg win and the home players were rightly pleased at their efforts when the referee blew for time. City won the return 2–0 thus earning the right to a replay. There were no winners when the neutral venue was announced – Copenhagen – and a crowd of 12,100 saw the Blues win 3–1 and move into the semi-finals for the second successive year.

The draw pitted the Blues with the only other English team left, Chelsea, and the familiarity of the two clubs did no favours for either side. With a crippling injury list including Alan Oakes, Colin Bell, Mike Doyle, Glyn Pardoe and Mike Summerbee, City lost the first leg 1–0. Tommy Booth and Joe Corrigan were also absent from the second leg and a 1–0 defeat at Maine Road was hardly surprising. With a fit and full squad, Mercer's side may well have gone on to win the Cup Winners' Cup again, but, alas, we'll never know.

EVER PRESENTS

The player who holds the record for appearing in every league game in a season the most times is winger Eric Brook (1928–40), who on five occasions played in all the matches in a season – hardly a shock that he also holds the record of consecutive appearances, too. Joe Corrigan (1967–83), Billy Meredith (1894–1905) and Frank Swift (1932–49) are three legendary figures that each have had a total four seasons of never having missed a game. Steve Redmond (1984–92), with three full seasons of playing, is the most recent in the list. It seems, with the phrase 'squad rotation' becoming more and more a by-word in the modern game – especially among the bigger clubs – that being an ever-present these days is quite an achievement.

UP FOR THE CUP – GLORY

Winners on five occasions and finalists on another four visits to Wembley, City have done fairly well in the FA Cup over the past 116 years. The first time the Blues lifted the trophy was in 1904 when a narrow 1–0 win over Bolton at the Crystal Palace softened the blow of finishing runners-up in Division One and thus missing a historic double. Bolton, unfortunately, would have their revenge in 1926, winning the cup by scoring the game's only goal in City's first-ever Wembley appearance. Seven years after that, City were again on the losing side, this time to Everton. Determined to get it right, Wilf Wild's side returned the following year to lift the cup for the second time after beating Portsmouth 2–1, under captain Sam Cowan's inspirational leadership.

History repeated itself in 1955 when City went down 3–1 to Newcastle United only to go all the way the next year and win the competition 3–1 over Birmingham City. It would be 1969 before City returned to the Twin Towers – a Neil Young thunderbolt giving Joe Mercer's side a 1–0 victory over Leicester. The last appearance in the final for a while by a Manchester City team was in 1981 when Tottenham triumphed 3–2 in a replayed match after the first game ended 1–1. There were memorable goals by Tommy Hutchison, Steve Mackenzie and Ricky Villa over the two matches, watched by a combined attendance of 192,500. The 2010/11 FA Cup campaign saw City end their 35-year wait to win a trophy when the Blues beat Stoke 1–0 courtesy of Yaya Touré's 74th-minute strike.

GIANT KILLED

City, playing the role of giants, have been slain on several occasions over the years and there will never be a match against lower league opposition that doesn't give City fans the willies. Top of the disaster pile would have to be the 1980 third-round defeat at Fourth Division Halifax Town. The Blues, managed by Malcolm Allison, must have thought The Shay was hell on earth as they ran out into a dilapidated stadium and a glue-pot of a pitch. With record signing Steve Daley probably worth more than the entire Halifax team – and ground – failing to inspire City, the game looked to be heading for a 0–0 draw. Then, with ten minutes to go, Halifax striker Paul Hendrie tucked away a low drive that proved enough to fell the once mighty Blues. Malcolm Allison later claimed the stain of the result would never be forgotten: the game is replayed on third-round day year after year – the public loves watching a good flogging.

City had 'previous', though, and the year before, City had gone to Third Division Shrewsbury Town and lost 2–0 on a rock-solid frosty pitch at Gay Meadow. Further embarrassments included a 2–1 defeat at Blackpool in 1984, a 3–1 loss to Brentford in 1989 and a 1–0 reverse at Cardiff City in 1994. In the League Cup, in recent years Doncaster Rovers and Chesterfield have piled on the agony, with both opposition sides knocking out the Premiership giants while earning a crust in League One (Division Three in days of yore).

WRITE ON BRIGADE

The first and longest-surviving fanzine is Dave Wallace's *King of the Kippax* – the broadsheet of the City fanzines – and it'll be a sad day when Dave and his team of helpers are absent from whichever ground the Blues are playing at. Noel Bayley's now-defunct *Bert Trautmann's Helmet* was well produced and a little more vociferous with its opinions, while *City 'til I Cry* and *Chips and Gravy* have appeared over the past few seasons and have been well received in a surprisingly competitive market.

Among the all-time best, the now-defunct *Blue Print* played a huge part in the late 1980s plastic banana invasion and its editor Bill Borrows was responsible for the sole issue (to date) of *Time Out Manchester*. Also gone, but not forgotten, are *Main Stand View*, *This Charming Fan* and *Blue Murder*. Credit is due to the fanzine editors for the hard work and efforts they put in for little reward. Standing on corners on match days in the pouring rain is no fun but it goes with the territory. There is no shortage of talent among their editors and contributors, either, and long may they continue (so long as they give this book a good review).

DOMESTICALLY WORST WINNERS

The Blues hold the record for being worst domestically finishing side to have won the European Cup Winners' Cup, having finished in tenth in 1969/70. The league record that season was:

P 42   W16   D 11   L 15   F 55   A 48   Pts 43

EURO CURRENCIES

Joe Corrigan holds the record for European appearances with 27, while Tommy Booth made 26 starts, Colin Bell 23 and Mike Doyle and Franny Lee played for the Blues in 22 ties. Franny Lee is the top scorer with 10 goals, Bell is second with 8 and Brian Kidd has scored 6.

THE SHINY SHOW

The four floodlight pylons that used to tower over Maine Road and the surrounding area for decades were eventually replaced by sophisticated lighting from the top of the Kippax and Main Stand. The four iron constructions had been in place since 1953 and caused City fans who ever stood close to them to think the same thought as they gazed up at the never-ending ladder that sometimes seemed to disappear into the low-lying cloud base: 'Thank God I don't have to change the light bulbs!'

The floodlights were first turned on for a friendly against Hearts on 14 October 1953. The Blues wore special 'shiny shirts' for the evening and won an entertaining game 6–3 in front of a healthy 23,979 crowd. With good comes bad and the innovative lighting brought Manchester United back to Maine Road to play various friendlies and cup games until Old Trafford had their own installed in 1957. Not, however, before Maine Road became the first English ground to play host to a European Cup match in 1956 – and the Blues weren't even involved! United beat RSC Anderlecht 10–0 in a close-fought game.

LEAGUE CUP GLORY

There was a time when City threatened to dominate this competition, which has been given a series of oddly sponsored titles over the past 20 years or so, including the Milk Cup, Rumbelows Cup, Littlewoods Cup, Coca-Cola Cup, Worthington Cup and Carling Cup. The trophy came into existence in 1960 and City's first-ever game was a 3–0 win over Stockport County. Four years later and Stoke

City defeated the Blues over two legs in the semi-final on aggregate by 2–1.

In 1969/70, the Cup finally found its way into the Maine Road trophy room. Victories over Southport, Liverpool, Everton and QPR set up a semi-final with United over two legs. City won 2–1 at Maine Road but trailed by the same score in the return leg with minutes left on the clock. The referee awarded City an indirect free kick on the edge of the Reds' box and Franny Lee took a crack at goal. Alex Stepney could have stepped aside and the goal wouldn't have counted but instinct got the better of him and he parried the thunderous drive to Mike Summerbee, who tucked away the equaliser. In the final, a tired City side (they had recently played a grueling European Cup Winners' Cup match) slogged it out against West Bromwich Albion on a glue-pot of a pitch and it took an extra-time winner from Glyn Pardoe to settle affairs.

City returned in 1974 under Ron Saunders, but lost 2–1 to Wolves with Colin Bell the scorer. Two years later and City dispatched Norwich City, Nottingham Forest, Manchester United, Mansfield Town and Middlesbrough to earn the right to play Newcastle United at Wembley. Peter Barnes opened the scoring before Alan Gowling levelled for the Magpies. The best was yet to come and Dennis Tueart's overhead goal spectacularly won the game 2–1 for the Blues. In 1980/81 John Bond's side met Liverpool in the last four, controversially losing 2–1 over two legs. In 2009/10, City played Manchester United over two legs for the right to play in the final and City won the first leg 2–1 thanks to two Carlos Tevez goals. Sadly, the Reds won the return game 3–1 to progress to Wembley at our expense.

MAINE MEN

The Football Writers' Footballer of the Year award has been won on three occasions by City players. In 1955 the press recognised the intelligent role Don Revie had adopted in the City team where he played as a deep-lying forward for the team. Bert Trautmann won the award the following year after his courageous display in the 1956 FA Cup final, playing on despite having a broken neck, to help his side beat Birmingham City 3–1. In 1969 it was Tony Book who received the honour by his peers as he collected the PFA award (sharing with Derby County's Dave Mackay) – this despite having a serious knee injury that had kept him out for most of the season.

FOREIGN PLAYERS

The first foreign player on City's books is believed to have been Canadian Walter Bowman, who toured with his national side in 1891 and subsequently decided he liked the area so much that he signed for Ardwick FC. He made 49 starts and scored three goals in eight years.

City's links with Holland stretch back before the First World War with Dutch international Nico Bouvy playing two reserve games before returning home. Former prisoner-of-war Bert Trautmann became one of the Blues' best goalkeepers ever, with the big German giving the Blues fifteen years of superb service. Gerry Baker was born in New York and signed in 1960 from St Mirren. He scored a total of 14 goals in 39 games before returning to Scotland with Hibs a year later.

Colin Viljoen remains the only South African to have played for the Blues and Kaziu Deyna is still the only Polish star to have graced the light blue shirt. Since Deyna, there have been many nationalities play for City and if there are others out there like Georgi Kinkladze, Ali Benarbia or Eyal Berkovic, long may they continue to come – after 2007, the list expanded to the extent we'd need a whole chapter just for the foreign talent that has represented the club. Robinho, Carlos Tevez, Yaya Touré and David Silva are among the biggest names in recent times.

FULL MEMBERS' CUP

Though the club entered this much-maligned and crude-sounding competition on several occasions, it was in 1985/86 – the first time City had been involved – which made an impression in the minds of Blues followers. Considered as little more than a joke by most of the football world, both the Blues and Chelsea plugged away through the rounds in front of sparse crowds to reach the final at Wembley.

The press had a field day poking fun at the competition's poor image, and despite both clubs having to play a league match the day before, when 68,000 fans turned out on the day the only people laughing were the chairmen of both clubs. The final itself was a terrific advert for the game. City led 1–0 through Mark Lillis, but the Pensioners roared back with vengeance to lead 5–1. With minutes left, City pulled three goals back through Lillis, Kinsey and an own goal to narrowly lose 5–4. The Blues never again reached such heights in the competition and their last appearance was in 1991/92 when two Colin Hendry goals weren't enough to beat Sheffield Wednesday, who won 3–2. Like anyone cared . . .

DON'T MENTION THE WAR

The links between City and Germany are possibly stronger than at any other club in Britain. The ties stretch back to 1949, when, shortly after the Second World War, former German paratrooper Bert Trautmann was signed, somewhat controversially, by manager Jock Thomson. Trautmann was understudy to the great Frank Swift, but eventually took over and soon won the respect of the fans with his courageous displays.

Few people are likely to be aware that midfielder David Phillips (1984–86) was born in Wegberg, Germany – though he represented Wales at international level – and Northern Irish international Steve Lomas was born in the British Army stronghold of Hanover. In March 1994 Brian Horton signed Uwe Rosler and then brought in Stefan Karl on loan until the end of the season. Rosler was an instant hit with the fans and led the forward line for four highly productive years. South American-looking Maurizio Gaudino became the sixth German-born player to represent City and became another firm crowd favourite during his six-month loan spell from Eintracht Frankfurt. Eike Immel became only City's second-ever German goalkeeper when he arrived at Maine Road in 1995. He was an ever present during his first full season but lost his place the following year and returned to his homeland. Full-back Michael Frontzeck failed to settle – or impress – and he proved the least successful of all the club's German recruits. Michael Tarnat enjoyed a productive season with City in 2003/04 and scored several spectacular goals. Finally, former City manager Kevin Keegan played for SV Hamburg and helped them win the European Cup during his stay. 'Mighty Mouse' is still considered something of an icon by the SV fans some 20-plus years on, and a crowd of 30,000 turned up to welcome him back for a friendly in August 2002.

BHOYS WILL BE BHOYS

Though City and Celtic have met on eleven occasions, the sides have never met competitively. The first of the friendly games dates back to 1891, with Celtic leaving Manchester with a 1–0 win. By 1903, the sides had played each other seven times in what was becoming an almost annual event and that year the Blues visited Parkhead for the first time, drawing 0–0. A large crowd witnessed another no-scoring draw at Parkhead in 1970 and the last meeting was in 1992, with Celtic winning 3–1 on neutral soil. The last meeting between the sides was in 2009 when the teams shared a 1–1 draw.

City's record against Celtic is:
Pld: 11   W: 3   D: 5   L: 3   F: 9   A: 14

POWER RANGERS

Out of the two Glasgow clubs, the links between City and Rangers are traditionally stronger, but City have actually played the Gers on fewer occasions than they have Celtic. The first meeting was in 1900 and Rangers won 3–0 at Hyde Road. A meeting at Ibrox saw City lose 2–0 in 1981. A Rangers and Celtic combined team – imagine that ever happening today – drew 2–2 at Maine Road in 1925 as part of a testimonial. In 2009, City played Rangers as part of their pre-season arrangements, losing 3–2.

City's record against Rangers is:
Pld: 9   W: 3   D: 1   L: 5   F: 14   A: 16

NET BUSTERS

The top ten goal-scorers, taking into account league goals only, are as follows:

1.	Eric Brook (1928–40)	159
2.	Tom Johnson (1919–30)	158
3.	Billy Meredith (1894–1906 & 1921–4)	145
4.	Joe Hayes (1953–65)	142
5.	Billy Gillespie (1897–1905)	126
6.	Tommy Browell (1913–26)	122
7.	Horace Barnes (1914–24)	120
8.	Colin Bell (1966–79)	117
9.	Frank Roberts (1922–9)	116
10.	Francis Lee (1967–74)	112

THE CLUB FORMERLY KNOWN AS …

When West Gorton and Gorton Athletic joined forces in 1883/84, a decision on the club's new name was taken and it became Gorton Association Football Club, the forerunner of Ardwick FC and eventually Manchester City FC. Gorton AFC played the majority of their home games at Pink Bank Lane, but later moved to Reddish Lane.

GOLDEN GOAL

City used to have their own version of the Golden Goal rule, sometimes applied in certain cup competitions. A unique stamped four-figure number would be inside the match-day programme and when the first goal was scored, the number of seconds was calculated and that was the Golden Goal time. It was easy to identify the winner after a 0–0 draw because there was always one lucky programme with '0000'. The winner won £100 in its heyday.

ON WHAT GROUNDS?

Encompassing all the names the club has played under since its inception in 1880, the following is a list of the grounds that, at some point or other, the club called home:

1880–1	Clowes Street
1881–2	Kirkmanshulme Lane Cricket Club
1882–4	Queens Road
1884–5	Pink Bank Lane
1885–7	The Bull's Head Hotel, Reddish Lane
1887–1923	Hyde Road
1923–2003	Maine Road
2003–present	City of Manchester Stadium

MAKE MINE A TREBLE

Billy Meredith, Fred Tilson and Tommy Browell have all scored six hat-tricks for City in the league and Irvine Thornley scored five. There was only one occasion when three players scored a hat-trick for City in the same game and that was when Huddersfield Town lost 10–1 at Maine Road in 1987. Tony Adcock, Paul Stewart and David White all scored three times that afternoon – only the fifth time in Football League history that such a feat has been achieved.

Ken Barnes scored three penalties in a 6–2 win over Everton in 1957 while Dennis Tueart was something of a hat-trick specialist. In 1977/78 he scored three in a 4–1 win at Villa Park, another three in a 6–2 win over Chelsea in November of the same year, and he made it three hat-tricks in five months with another in a 4–0 win over Newcastle United on Boxing Day 1977. Carlos Tevez had managed three trebles up to April 2011 against West Brom, Wigan and Blackburn.

NAVY BLUES

A particularly strong City Youth side beat naval HMS *Manchester* in August 1985 by 13–0. The prolific Paul Moulden demonstrated his predatory instincts by scoring five goals in 20 minutes with the naval defence apparently all at sea.

HOME IS WHERE THE HEART IS

City's record league home win was 11–3 against Lincoln City in March 1895 in Division Two. In a tight encounter, City beat Liverpool Stanley (who are they?) 12–0 in October 1890 during an FA Cup qualifying round and in February 1926 the Blues thrashed Crystal Palace 11–4 in the fifth round of the FA Cup – they totaled 30 goals on their way to the final, which they lost to Bolton 1–0! Three more occasions resulted in City reaching double figures. In 1898/99, Darwen returned home after a 10–0 drubbing in a Division Two fixture and City once hit Swindon Town for ten in the FA Cup with the visitors replying once. The most recent double-figures win was during a Division Two game in November 1987 when City hammered Huddersfield Town 10–1.

There have also been three 9–0 wins: Burton Swifts in 1897/98, Gainsborough Trinity in 1902/03 and Gateshead in 1932/33. On the flip side, West Bromwich Albion's 7–2 win at Maine Road on New Year's Day 1934 remains the Blues' heaviest-ever home loss. The Blues have completed four unbeaten seasons at home and only one of them has been at Maine Road. The seasons are: 1895/96 (Division Two), 1904/05 (Division Two), 1920/21 (Division One) and 1965/66 (Division Two).

HYDE AND SEEK

Now the site of a Manchester bus company, Hyde Road was City's first enclosed ground and was home to Ardwick FC from 1887 to 1894 and then Manchester City FC from 1894 until 1923. The ground was hemmed in by a railway track to the west and sidings to the north – train drivers would often slow down to catch a glimpse of City in action! Crowds were only estimated at the time and ranged from 500 to 40,000 and the Blues were Division One runners-up on two occasions while at the ground, but with the team's popularity growing rapidly it became clear that a new home was desperately needed. The need for a new home cranked up a couple of notches after the Main Stand burned down in 1920. Belle Vue, a few miles up the road, was cited as a possible home, but the eight-acre plot was not nearly big enough to house the club.

A space was found in Moss Side, several miles away, and the foundations of a new stadium were soon visible to curious supporters. In the summer of 1923, Maine Road was completed and City closed the gates at Hyde Road for the last time. The Main Stand roof was sold to Halifax Town for the princely sum of £1,000 and was still standing when the Blues lost 1–0 at The Shay in 1980. Today, the area the pitch once occupied is now a skid pan for training bus drivers in Bennett Street – there must be a joke in there somewhere. . . .

INTERNATIONAL RESCUE

There were only a couple of international matches at Maine Road since the Second World War and England enjoyed a 100 per cent record for their appearances in Moss Side. The first time the national squad played at City's home ground was on 13 November 1946, when they beat Wales 3–0. Just over three years later, on 16 November 1949, England crushed Northern Ireland 9–2 in a World Cup qualifier. There have been numerous England Under-21 games played at the ground, many during the late 1970s when the side was sprinkled with talented City youngsters such as Barnes and Owen. As Wembley lay in a state of disrepair, England played two matches at the City of Manchester Stadium in 2004, beating Iceland 6–1 and Japan 2–0.

GET THEM WHILE THEY'RE YOUNG

City were the first club to set up a junior supporters' club, the Junior Blues, and it proved to be the role model that other clubs aspired to over the following years. Based loosely around an idea by Malcolm Allison, the project came to light under the chairmanship of Peter Swales in 1973. The rules were simple – discipline and good behaviour towards each other and other youngsters, particularly from other clubs, and to have as much fun as possible. The success of the Junior Blues led to other clubs – believed to be as many as 70 – contacting the Blues for advice and guidance to enhance their own junior schemes. In 2006 the club launched a new initiative – LIVE4CITY – which continued the good work started by the Junior Blues but with a whole new range of incentives and goals.

WE ARE THE KIPPAX!

Home to thousands of City fans since 1923, the famous, much-loved old terrace was often the extra man for the Blues as the supporters roared them on to success. It could also mean the end of a player if the poor soul wasn't performing well over a period of time. Many an opposing winger has turned a pasty shade of white at the sight of a packed, baying and swaying Kippax terrace.

It was over 35 years before a roof was erected to keep the regular Mancunian drizzle off the supporters' heads and, with a smart new covering, the side of the ground known as the 'popular side' was officially named the Kippax Stand after the street it was next to. It was home to 32,000 loyal Blues, though this was reduced to 26,155 when the North Stand was completed in 1971. Further reductions meant that only 18,300 City fans stood in the cavernous old stand by the time of its eventual demise.

It would be impossible to say how many times City fans have actually stood on the terrace, but a safe estimate would be several million. The Taylor Report, a government-backed investigation into the safety of standing areas at football grounds, recommended that all terracing become seated areas, which effectively signaled the end for the Kippax as a terraced stand. City supporters paid their final respects to their favourite part of the ground on 30 April 1994 when City took on Chelsea. Fancy dress, flags and balloons festooned the Kippax and celebrated its 71-year life. Many shed a tear after the final whistle and attempted to chip bits of concrete off steps as a souvenir.

A couple of days later, the demolition teams moved in and pictures appeared in the local media of rubble and steel girders where the Kippax had once stood proudly. From the dust arose the new Kippax, three tiers high and visible for miles around. The new stand was opened to City fans for the first home game of the 1995/96 season. Many fans groaned as they took their seats in the second and third tier on first inspection – nothing to do with the perfect view of the pitch, but because Old Trafford was now visible in the distance! The New Kippax soon found itself victim to the bulldozers when Maine Road was levelled over a period of several months between 2003 and 2004.

HOT SEAT SHENANIGANS

Up to and including Stuart Pearce, manager of City for the start of the 2006/07 campaign, the Blues had 33 managers in 116 years. This doesn't take into account caretaker managers, such as Asa Hartford, Tony Book, Phil Neal, Ken Barnes and others. Each full-time boss has obviously had varied lengths of time either through choice or otherwise. The longest to survive in the hot seat is Wilf Wild, who managed the club from 1932 to 1946. Les McDowall was in charge for 13 years and Ernest Mangnall was at the helm for 12 years.

The shortest period of time was Steve Coppell's month-long reign in 1996. The club's reputation for something of a merry-go-round of managerial appointments stems from the time John Bond quit in 1983. Twelve bosses in 18 years equate to an average of 18 months for each boss. The overall average is three years and six months. Before 1983, it was an average of almost five years in the manager's chair.

DO GO NEAR THE MAINE ROAD

Home to Manchester City from 1923 to 2003, the club finally ended its tenure in Manchester 14 with a 1–0 home loss to Southampton on 11 May 2003. The Blues played at their new home in 1923, just four months after Wembley Stadium was completed, after leaving Hyde Road and its limited capacity. Designed by local architect Charles Swain, the original plan was for the ground to match Wembley and hold 90,000 spectators – 'a stadium fit for Manchester's premier club' as stated by officials at the time.

The opening game in August 1923 introduced the fans to this huge arena and many were in awe of its size. With only the Main Stand's 10,000 seats covered, the rest of the ground was open terracing. Buoyed on by a record crowd of 56,993, the Blues beat Sheffield United 2–1 with goals from Tom Johnson and Horace Barnes. The next home game proved that the new ground was sadly not impregnable and City lost 2–1 to Aston Villa, though the club would lose just twice more at home that season.

The 'popular side', later known as the Kippax, had a flagpole positioned roughly level with the halfway line at the very back of the terracing. Before each home game, a member of staff would proudly raise the club flag with 'City FC' on and then lower it after the match had ended.

Surprisingly, City have only once gone an entire league season at Maine Road without defeat. This was when the club went up as Second Division Champions in the 1965/66 campaign. For 17 months the Blues were undefeated at home in the league. Maine Road's four stands were all full of character and had their own personality and traditions, even if none of them matched: the North Stand (formerly the Scoreboard End), Platt Lane and the Main Stand (though the Kippax housed the majority of die-hards). Developed at different stages over a number of years, the four stands gave the stadium an unusual and unique look.

None of the four roofs linked up and because of the all-seater stadia ruling, there were capacity issues that forced the club to seek out a new home, which was why in 2003 the club packed up lock, stock and barrel and moved across town to East Manchester and the City of Manchester Stadium. Despite the emotional attachment of the City faithful who have bared their souls to the concrete and steel that makes up Maine Road, they were fully behind the change of ground. When all is said and done, City have only won the Division One Championship twice while in Moss Side and for all the happy memories, the ground held equal measures of disappointment, despair and heartbreak. Maine Road will remain in each fan's heart for many years to come and forever be regarded as the Blues' spiritual home.

HEL'S BELLS

It was once tradition for a tracksuited youngster to run out before the Blues came on at Maine Road and run around the perimeter of the pitch. Youngster Paul Todd was lucky to get the job permanently for a few years during City's golden era during the late 1960s. There have always been kids that walk on the pitch with the City players and have a kick-around with one of the players but, as for official club mascots, 'Moonchester' was the first real mascot City had. The blue alien is popular with the kids and in December 2001 the club introduced 'Moonbeam', Moonchester's female companion.

Most clubs have a mascot; the most memorable for many City fans was 'Mr Posh', the mascot of Peterborough United. Thousands of Blues had made the journey for an FA Cup fifth round tie at London Road and poor old Mr Posh came in for the royal treatment as he passed the packed City enclosure complete with monocle and top hat. Talk about sitting ducks! It was all good fun, of course.

The banana craze of the late 1980s could also be considered an unofficial kind of mascot – the City players ran out at Stoke City with giant bananas on Boxing Day 1988 as a tribute to the fans but it didn't help the team too much as they went down 3–1. Another unofficial mascot was Helen Turner, AKA 'Big Helen', who used to sit on the front row of the North Stand, presenting Joe Corrigan with a lucky sprig of heather prior to kick-off and ring a cow bell during times when the Blues needed a lift. She was kept very busy most of the time.

NO-ONE LIKES THEM

For some reason that is unclear, City and Millwall are not the best of friends. Crowd trouble flared during City's visit to the New Den in 1998 when Lee Bradbury equalised for the Blues in the last minute to earn a 1–1 draw from a bad-tempered affair. Chaos ensued outside the ground as the home fans laid siege to the travelling army in disgraceful scenes that are all too common with certain factions of the

Lions' support. The return game saw around 2,500 Millwall fans tearing seats up in the North Stand as their team was roundly beaten 3–0. Trouble flared outside the ground before and after the match with many innocents caught in the middle. With Millwall and City once again in the same division for the 2001/02 season, the clubs wisely agreed that there could be no repeat of the violence and took the unusual step of banning the away fans from each fixture. City won 3–2 at Millwall and Darren Huckerby applauded the empty stand that should have housed the City fans after his goal to the delight of the thousands watching on a huge screen back at Maine Road. The Blues reciprocated the ban and won the return 2–0.

RECORD-BREAKER

Arguably one of the finest prospects ever to play at any level for Manchester City, Paul Moulden, many believe, should have become a striker regarded in the same bracket as Robbie Fowler or Michael Owen. Signed from Bolton Boys, the Blues fought off a whole host of clubs eager to take the young forward on. His scoring exploits at schoolboy level is the stuff of legend and he is officially entered in the *Guinness Book of Records* after netting an unbelievable 289 times in 40 matches – an average of just over 7 per game! He scored 12 goals in 13 FA Youth Cup games for City and picked up a winners' medal along the way and finished top scorer in the reserves for three out of four seasons. He forced his way into the first team on New Year's Day 1986 and played his part in a 1–0 away win at Aston Villa. A couple more games here and there in 1986/87 and then Jimmy Frizzell gave him a longer run and he scored four in four games at one point in a side destined for relegation. A broken leg – one of four leg breaks in his City career – kept his progress on hold under Mel Machin's reign but for the 1988/89 campaign he ended top scorer making 29 starts and scoring 13 goals as City gained promotion. He left for Bournemouth in June 1989. The glittering career that had once beckoned was all but ruined by injury and today the boy wonder runs a fish and chip shop. He deserved much batter (geddit?).

BLUE MOVIES

Though some of City's escapades would have lent themselves well to a Hollywood disaster movie adaptation, there have been a couple of moments of real movie stardom for City stars in the past. Mike Summerbee was in *Escape to Victory* and can therefore truthfully claim he has played alongside Pelé and Sylvester Stallone in the same 90 minutes! Polish star Kaziu Deyna was also featured in the movie. Colin Bell wasn't in the classic *Italian Job* but a flag draped out of a white van with his name on was featured in the movie. It's doubtful he received any royalties. The film *There's Only One Jimmy Grimble*, starring Robert Carlyle and Ray Winstone, was based around a young boy and his dream to one day play for Manchester City. Many scenes were filmed in and around Maine Road and the final portion featured Jimmy Grimble finally realising his dream and playing on the hallowed turf. It was never made, but *Bend it Like Benarbia* would have gone down a storm with the blue half of Manchester. Documentary *Blue Moon Rising* enjoyed a theatrical release in the summer of 2010 to rave reviews.

NO PLACE LIKE HOME – LITERALLY

Maine Road has played host to a number of games that didn't involve the Blues. Manchester United played many times in Moss Side after Old Trafford was bombed during the Second World War and there have been several FA Cup semi-finals held at the ground prior to the Kippax becoming an all-seater stand. A memorable game from the late 1970s involved non-league Altrincham FC, who took on Tottenham in an FA Cup replay. Having held the north Londoners to a 1–1 draw at White Hart Lane, a large crowd containing thousands of City fans saw Spurs win the game 3–0. Several rugby league games of varying importance were also held at Maine Road and international rugby league matches have already taken place at the City of Manchester Stadium.

WHICH DIVISION ARE YOU IN?

Given the history and tradition of Manchester City, nobody should be surprised that the Blues have, when the rare occasion has arisen, struggled to beat non-league opposition. All five games have, of course, been in the FA Cup. The early fixtures are harder to gauge, as non-league in the late 1890s didn't necessarily mean 'duff' opponents – hence Fleetwood Rangers drawing 1–1 and then winning the replay 2–0 in 1892. A year later West Manchester won 3–0 to send the club crashing out. Wigan County became the first minnows to succumb to the Blues by 1–0 and it would be 73 years before City would face non-leaguers again when in 1971 they scraped past Wigan Athletic 1–0, with Colin Bell scoring the only goal in front of 46,212 fans at Maine Road. The Blues have never drawn a non-league club since.

DROLL WITH IT

Burnage-born brothers Noel and Liam Gallagher, the driving forces behind defunct rock band Oasis, are famously also lifelong City supporters, though their matchday attendance has become infrequent since they took up residency in London. During the mid-1990s, the band and the club seemed to merge into one with the same style of branding, followers and fashion. City ran out to 'Roll with It' for a while and it was rare for an Oasis record not to be playing during the half-time break at Maine Road. The Gallaghers were happy to promote the Blues by wearing the new shirts or mentioning their allegiances whenever they could during interviews. On at least two occasions the lads have walked out on to the pitch to the acclaim of the City faithful. Noel even has 'MCFC' on one of his guitars.

In 1995 the City support turned their classic 'Wonderwall' into a swooning tribute to Kinkladze and, wait for it, Alan Ball, though Noel commented that he wasn't too happy about the Alan Ball verse. The culmination of mutual admiration between band and club reached epidemic proportions when Oasis played several sold-out gigs at Maine Road. Once touted as potential owners, Noel agreed during the Division One Championship celebrations to record a version of 'Blue Moon' at Kevin Keegan's request but later said that he'd been drunk and would probably have agreed to anything and ultimately didn't play. The band returned to Manchester to play a series of sold-out concerts at the City of Manchester Stadium in 2005 but split up in 2010 due to irreconcilable differences between the warring siblings.

ONE-MATCH WONDERS

There have been 53 'one-match wonders' for City since the club first formed. The majority of these were during the First World War when things were slightly different regarding who played where and how often. The list is composed of players who started a league or cup match for the Blues on one occasion only. Substitutes are under another section. The most notable of these singular stars is probably former Northern Irish international Neil Lennon. The flame-haired midfielder played his one and only game for City's first team on 30 April 1988 as a promising, inexperienced teenager. City won the game away to Birmingham City 3–0. Lennon moved to Leicester City and later to Celtic for £5 million.

Five of the 53 managed to find the net on their only appearance. B. Campbell scored two goals in a 12–0 FA Cup qualifier in 1890 and never played for the club again. A. Spittle was the second to achieve the feat in 1894 as City lost 2–1 at home to Crewe Alexandra. J. Dennison bagged two goals during a 5–2 win over Blackburn Rovers in 1904. S. Eyres scored a goal in the final game of the 1906/07 season in a 3–2 home defeat by Sunderland and never played again, and F. Gorringe scored twice in a 7–3 home win over Barnsley on 2 January 1928 before disappearing into the sunset.

OH S***!

Dave Ewing holds an unenviable record that will probably never be beaten. With ten own goals during his playing career, nobody even comes close to taking away his unwanted crown. John McTavish scored three past his own goalkeeper in just four games in November 1959 – how many black cats must he have run over to earn such rotten luck? Derek Kevan and Steve Mackenzie both scored at either end for the Blues; Kevan's came in a 4–3 defeat at Charlton in 1964 and Mackenzie's dubious double was at Middlesbrough in 1980, with the game ending 2–2.

The most famous own goal of all was also one of the most painful. Tommy Hutchison's flying header had put City 1–0 up in the 1981 FA Cup final but he deflected a Spurs free kick past Joe Corrigan to become the only man to score at both ends in an FA Cup final – a record that still stands. The Blues' history might have been different had Dave Watson not bizarrely slid the ball past his own goalkeeper with two minutes to go of a crucial game against Liverpool. City had been leading 1–0 and the Merseyside Reds ended up winning the title five months later by a point over the Blues. The positions would have been reversed but for the fateful Watson error and City would have been champions for the second time in eight years. Richard Dunne put eight own goals past various City keepers and Kevin Bond notched a couple during his time with City.

Finally, the most entertaining of all the own goals ever scored came in a non-competitive match for Bert Trautmann's testimonial. A combined City and United team took on an International XI before a crowd of more than 48,000. United's Maurice Setters, playing in sky blue for the first and only time, received the ball and headed towards his own goal, kept by Trautmann. Setters then promptly tucked it past the German legend and ran off celebrating. His explanation was that he'd never managed to score against Trautmann before and this match represented his last opportunity. 'I couldn't resist it!' he added.

HOWDY, PARTNER

Some of the best striking partnerships City have had are as follows (goals in all competitions):

58	Roberts (30) and Browell (28)	1925/26
57	Goater (32) and Huckerby (25)	2001/02
57	Kevan (36) and Murray (21)	1963/64
54	Doherty (32) and Brook (22)	1936/37
52	Meredith (22) and Gillespie (30)	1902/03
52	Johnson (38) and Brook (14)	1928/29
52	Tait (31) and Marshall (21)	1929/30
49	Lee (35) and Bell (14)	1971/72
48	Browell (31) and Barnes (17)	1920/21
48	Stewart (28) and Varadi (20)	1987/88
48	Meredith (30) and Gillespie (18)	1898/99
47	Johnson (25) and Hicks (22)	1926/27
47	Halliday (32) and Marshall (15)	1931/32
46	Browell (26) and Barnes (20)	1921/22
46	Westcott (25) and Smith (21)	1950/51
45	Barnes (23) and Browell (22)	1919/20
45	Hayes (26) and McAdams (19)	1957/58
44	Roberts (32) and Johnson (12)	1924/25

PAYING THE PENALTY

Ask most City fans and they will tell you they just don't trust one of their players to score from the spot. By tracing back through history, the origins of uncertainty are easier to understand and by passing on the fear, generation after generation have inherited their parents' pessimism.

For instance, in 1912, City managed to miss three penalties in one game! Irvine Thornley and Eli Fletcher (twice) were the guilty parties and the game with Newcastle ended 1–1. It was back to St James' Park for another unfortunate day from the spot, this time for Billy Austin, when in 1926, the Blues, who needed a point to avoid relegation after five successive wins, missed from the spot and lost 3–2 and were subsequently relegated. On a brighter note, Ken Barnes scored a hat-trick of penalties against Everton in December 1957 in a 6–2 victory and scored another in the return fixture at Goodison Park.

Franny Lee is the club's most successful penalty-taker ever with 46 spot-kicks successfully dispatched in his time at Maine Road. Lee won many of the penalties himself and earned the nickname 'Lee One Pen'. Dennis Tueart scored an impressive 24 times from the spot, including several double strikes.

Keith Curle scored nine times from the spot for City and Gio Kinkladze scored on seven occasions. Kevin Bond scored penalties in the 44th and 45th minutes of a home game against Huddersfield Town in April 1984 to bring the scores level at 2–2, but the Blues still lost 3–2. Kevin Reeves scored City's solitary Wembley penalty, awarded during 90 minutes in the 1981 FA Cup final replay with Spurs to put his side 2–1 up in the second half. Shaun Goater and Neil McNab have both missed last-minute kicks that would have turned draws into victories.

There was a controversial incident in March 1960 when Denis Law made his home debut against West Ham. Trailing 1–0, Law was fouled in the box and the Blues were awarded a penalty. Ken Barnes placed the ball on the spot, ran up and tapped it forward for Billy McAdams to run from behind and tuck the ball away. The referee gave the goal but amid furious protests from the Hammers, he consulted a linesman and ordered the kick to be retaken. Barnes stepped up again and missed! Fortunately, City went on to win 3–1. Carlos Tevez has taken penalties since 2009, missing two but converting more than a dozen by April 2011.

The list of the most successful takers is:

	Seasons	League	Cup	Total
1. Francis Lee	1967–74	34	12	46
2. Eric Brook	1928–40	29	6	35
3. Dennis Tueart	1974–8 & 1980–3	18	6	24
4. Tom Johnson	1919–30	20	1	21
5. Ken Barnes	1950–61	13	–	13

FIXED PENALTY

The dramatic 1999 play-off victory over Gillingham was the most famous penalty shoot-out City have ever featured in. With a place in Division One awaiting the winners, Kevin Horlock put City 1–0 ahead from the spot and after the Gills missed their first effort, Paul Dickov stepped up. His shot hit one post, rolled agonisingly along the line behind Vince Bartram and hit the other post before bouncing to safety. The Gills missed their second and Terry Cooke safely dispatched City's third penalty for a 2–0 lead. The Gills made it 2–1 and Richard Edghill stepped up for the crucial fourth. He confidently struck the ball against the underside of the bar for 3–1. Nicky Weaver saved the next penalty and City were promoted.

The only other occasions the Blues have been involved in shoot-outs were in 1997 when Blackpool and City each won their home leg of the Worthington Cup ties by 1–0 and couldn't be separated in extra time, but City eventually lost 4–2 on penalties. An even more dramatic shoot-out occurred in 1981, once again in the League Cup. After beating Stoke City 2–0 at Maine Road, the Blues lost the return by the same score and so began an epic shoot-out for the right to progress into the third round. Both teams were competent from the spot and with scores locked at 8–8, Joe Corrigan saved well to present substitute Aage Hareide the chance of being a hero. The Norwegian stepped up and coolly stroked the ball home for a 9–8 win.

The Blues' most recent penalty drama was in 2005 when they lost 3–0 to Doncaster after missing their first three spot-kicks – this despite scoring one in normal time!

PLASTIC OH NO (BANNED)

Like the majority of footballers, City players were glad to see the demise of the dreaded 'plastic pitch', or Astroturf if you want to be all Stars and Stripes about it. Of the four clubs that laid this monstrosity of a playing surface (QPR, Luton Town, Preston North End and Oldham Athletic), City played three out of the 'Plastic Quartet' in league matches. The Blues drew 0–0 at QPR in 1985/86 and lost 1–0 the following season. Four visits to Kenilworth Road, home of Luton Town, produced two draws and two defeats and the curse continued with a 1–1 draw with Oldham Athletic in 1987/88. It would take the debutant Gary Megson to lay the plastic bogey with the only goal of the following season's fixture between City and Latics. One win in eight games on the all-weather pitches – thank God, they're confined to history! They're no longer a valid reason for players to wear ladies' stockings for the afternoon (unless you are Ryan Giggs, of course).

RAGS TO RICHES

The highest-profile players to have played for both Manchester clubs at one level or another are as follows: Billy Meredith, Eric Westwood, Denis Law, Peter Barnes, Wyn Davies, Brian Kidd, John Gidman, Tony Coton, Andy Hill, Carlo Nash, Shaun Goater, Terry Cooke, Peter Schmeichel, Jon Macken and, of course, Carlos Tevez.

PLAYER OF THE YEAR

The list of Player of the Year awards that began following the completion of the 1966/67 season, as voted by the club's supporters, is as follows:

1966/67	Tony Book
1967/68	Colin Bell
1968/69	Glyn Pardoe
1969/70	Francis Lee
1970/71	Mike Doyle
1971/72	Mike Summerbee
1972/73	Mike Summerbee
1973/74	Mike Doyle
1974/75	Alan Oakes
1975/76	Joe Corrigan
1976/77	Dave Watson
1977/78	Joe Corrigan
1978/79	Asa Hartford
1979/80	Joe Corrigan
1980/81	Paul Power
1981/82	Tommy Caton
1982/83	Kevin Bond
1983/84	Mick McCarthy

1984/85	Paul Power
1985/86	Kenny Clements
1986/87	Neil McNab
1987/88	Steve Redmond
1988/89	Neil McNab
1989/90	Colin Hendry
1990/91	Niall Quinn
1991/92	Tony Coton
1992/93	Garry Flitcroft
1993/94	Tony Coton
1994/95	Uwe Rosler
1995/96	Gio Kinkladze
1996/97	Gio Kinkladze
1997/98	Michael Brown
1998/99	Gerard Wiekens
1999/2000	Shaun Goater
2000/01	Danny Tiatto
2001/02	Ali Benarbia
2002/03	Sylvain Distin
2003/04	Shaun Wright-Phillips
2004/05	Richard Dunne
2005/06	Richard Dunne
2006/07	Richard Dunne
2007/08	Richard Dunne
2008/09	Stephen Ireland
2009/10	Carlos Tevez
2010/11	Vincent Kompany

POINTS MAKE PRIZES, SOMETIMES

City's last two stays in Division One have produced record point hauls. In the 1999/2000 season a grand total of 89 points were gathered on the way to the Blues finishing runners-up to Charlton Athletic, while in 2001/02, Kevin

Keegan's men went ten better with a new club record – one of many achieved that season – of 99 points from 46 games. The fewest points a City side has ever managed was 18 from 28 games in 1893/94.

PREMIER LEAGUE

The formation of the English Premier League in time for the 1992/93 season coincided with a downward spiral in the fortunes of Manchester City that took a full decade to put right. Peter Reid guided his team to a respectable ninth place after finishing fifth the previous two seasons in the old Division One, but was then sacked the following season. Brian Horton found the going tough in his first season in the Maine Road hot seat, with City ending in sixteenth place and in the 1994/95 campaign, City finished one place lower, costing the unfortunate Horton his job. Alan Ball did worse still, managing the club during their first relegation from the Premiership by finishing one place lower still, in eighteenth. It was five seasons before Joe Royle took the club back to the top league but, alas, only for one season. Kevin Keegan guided City back to the top in 2002 and the Blues finished ninth at the first attempt, equaling the club's best finish up to that point. City finished two places off the relegation slots in 2003/04 before Stuart Pearce took the helm in March 2005 and guided the Blues to eighth, missing out on Europe by a point. City finished in fifteenth in Pearce's first full season in charge, thanks largely to a dismal second half of the campaign. In 2009/10, Roberto Mancini guided City to their then highest Premier League finish ever with the Blues ending in fifth place and in 2010/11 he broke that record by finishing third.

GOING UP!

City have won promotion 12 times, crowned as champions on seven occasions and once via the play-offs. The first occasion was achieved in 1898/99 when City ventured out of Division Two for the very first time after clinching their first piece of silverware. Four years later, City were champions again of Division Two for the 1902/03 season following relegation the season before. They achieved the feat for a third time in 1909/10, winning the Second Division after being relegated the season before. City's fourth second-tier championship was in 1927/28, they added a fifth in 1946/47 and in 1950/51 City were runners-up. Joe Mercer guided the team to its sixth Division Two title in 1965/66 and two years after they won the Division One Championship. In 1984/85 the Blues needed a win against Charlton to fend off Portsmouth's late challenge and for once, City delivered, winning 5–1 and clinching promotion. In 1988/89 City were runners-up in Division Two and in 1999 the Blues won promotion out of what was once known as Division Three and were promoted again in 2000 giving the club their only back-to-back promotions to date.

QUICKEST GOAL

Niall Quinn's goal after just 30 seconds against Bolton on 30 March 1996 is City's quickest Premiership goal on record. The fixture ended 1–1. Another Irishman, Stephen Ireland, scored after just 35 seconds of the UEFA Cup tie with Hamburg in April 2009.

DON'T MENTION THE 'R' WORD

City have been relegated eleven times so far with the very first demotion being in 1901/02 and it happened again in 1908/09, though on each occasion the club bounced back immediately after one season in Division Two.

Two cruel ironies coupled the next two relegations, proving that City are incapable of an average, run-of-the-mill disappointing season. In 1925/26 City lost 3–2 to Newcastle and missed a penalty on the final day, needing only a point to survive. The two clubs beneath, Leeds and Burnley, both won, sending the Blues down. With 89 goals scored during the ill-fated campaign, City still hold the record for the greatest amount of goals scored for a relegated club.

But the Blues hold the *coup de grâce* of all relegations having been relegated the season after they'd won the First Division Championship in 1936/37! This is another unwanted record the Blues hold. Other occasions when the Blues slipped out of the top flight were the 1949/50 and 1962/63 seasons. The 1980s were a miserable time for the club with further relegations in 1983 and 1987. Alan Ball took City down in 1996 and despite the final day 5–2 win at Stoke City in 1998, the Blues were relegated to Division Two. The 2000/01 relegation was the eleventh and last at the time.

THE MASTER PLAN

'The Revie Plan' centered around Don Revie, who signed for City in 1951 at a cost of £25,000. Playing as a deep-lying centre-forward, Revie was difficult to mark for defenders used to less inventive forwards. Though he only averaged around one goal every four games, Revie was able to make goals for others and confuse the opposition defence. So effective was he that he helped City to successive FA Cup finals in 1955 and 1956. It also brought him to the attention of England and he won six full caps.

However, the ill-fated 'Marsden Plan', centered around half-back Keith Marsden, was ditched after a 6–1 defeat to Preston and a 9–2 loss at West Brom!

EARLY BATH

Of the red cards shown to City players, some have been more memorable than others. In September 1962, Bert Trautmann was sent off for expressing dissent against West Ham at Maine Road. His dismissal saw the Blues collapse and lose 6–1. Ray Ranson and Tommy Booth were both sent off during a 'friendly' with Real Madrid in December 1979 and Mike Doyle once received his marching orders for punching Leighton James. Perhaps the best, or worst of all, depending on how you look at it, was Kevin Horlock's dismissal for 'walking aggressively'! Pablo Zabaleta has been sent off three times – against Wigan, Liverpool and Arsenal – up to April 2011. Italian striker Bernardo Corradi had two notable sendings off for City – his league debut at Chelsea in 2006 and his first Manchester derby a few months late, while Mario Balotelli received red cards against West Brom and Dynamo Kiev in 2010/11.

SEQUENCES

City's record for successive league wins is nine set between 8 April and 28 September 1912. Eight successive wins in one season have occurred twice in 1904/05 and 1946/47. The record for consecutive draws is five, set in 1899/1900 and repeated in 1951/52. City's worst run of defeats was set in 1995/96 when they lost eight on the trot under Alan Ball. The club has also suffered six consecutive defeats five times, in 1910/11, 1956/57, 1958/59 and 1960/61. The Blues went seventeen games without a win in the 1979/80 season – a run stretching nearly four months. The greatest number of games played without a draw – 20 – was set in 1892, ending in 1893. The club's longest unbeaten run – 22 games – was set first in 1936/37 and repeated a decade later in 1946/47.

ER, WE'RE NOT REALLY HERE

A largely embarrassing competition to be in, the Simod Cup's brief efforts to become the elusive third cup competition in England died away as the public's apathy grew with each passing game. The trophy, which changed names from Full Members' Cup to the Simod and Zenith Data Systems Cup, finally faded completely in the early 1990s. For the record, City played in the tournament for two seasons. The first Simod Cup tie, played in November 1987, saw City thrash Plymouth Argyle 6–2, just three days after hammering Huddersfield Town 10–1 in a Division Two fixture and City striker Tony Adcock scored a hat-trick in each game. The Blues went out in the next round 2–0 at home to Chelsea. In 1988, a 3–2 defeat by Blackburn Rovers at Ewood Park signaled the end of City's days in the cup.

CHANT NO. I

City supporters have sung many songs over the years but it wasn't until 1990 that 'Blue Moon' became the fans' anthem. Originally written by Richard Rodgers and Lorenz Hart, both Peterborough United and Crewe Alexandra claim they serenaded their respective teams with the anthem first but, as the old adage goes, if you're going to take somebody else's song, make it your own. Mention 'Blue Moon' to anybody today and they think of Manchester City, not Crewe or Peterborough. Sorry, boys, that's just the way it goes.

City's first national airing of the song was away to Aston Villa in an ITV live match from Villa Park on 1 April 1990. Suitably swept on a tide of emotion, the Blues won 2–1 and today no match involving City passes by without at least a couple of hearty renditions.

The 1970s were a great time for new songs and the Kippax favourites included the following: from the tune of 'Lily the Pink' came 'Colin the King' for Colin Bell; 'Sha-la-la-la-Summerbee' – self-explanatory; Dennis Tueart's song was 'Dennis Tueart King of all Geordies'; and 'Rodney, Rodney' for Rodney Marsh, who later admitted it gave him goose bumps every time he heard it.

There are more common and, in many cases, unprintable football songs heard at Maine Road but the ever-inventive Blues' fans were always coming up with originals like a customised version of the Oasis classic 'Wonderwall', 'I'm Dreaming of a Blue Wembley' and 'City 'til I Die'. The arrival of Shaun Goater, though, has spawned two favourite fan songs: 'Who Let the Goat Out?' and possibly one of the best ever, 'Feed the Goat (and he will score)', though the later was adapted to 'Feed the Greek and he will score!' in 2006 for Georgios Samaras. A challenger for best adaptation of a rubbish pop song ('Hey Mickey!' by Toni Basil) is 'Hey

Micah you're so fine, you scored a goal in added time, hey Micah! Hey Micah!' Adam Johnson, Pablo Zabaleta and Carlos Tevez all have their own chants and no doubt there will be many more to add to the list in future years.

NAME GAME

City have so far had five sponsors since club sponsorship began in time for the 1982/83 season. The first was Scandinavian car company Saab which used the Blues as a vehicle for three years during what would turn out to be one of the club's lowest ebbs. Much the same could be said of Dutch electronic giants Philips, owners of PSV Eindhoven. City achieved little while wearing their name on the front of the players' shirts. Brother's 10-year relationship was fruitful for both parties, with the Blues in the Premiership for much of the time. Electronic games giants Eidos were sponsors from 1998 to 2002. First Advice, a new financial advice company based in Manchester, became sponsors in July 2002 with the intention of a three-year deal, but they fell into financial difficulties and went belly up less than two years into the agreement. Thomas Cook then took up the slack for five years before the present shirt sponsors, Abu Dhabi airline Etihad, took over in 2009. The full list is:

1982–5	Saab
1985–8	Philips
1988–98	Brother
1998–2002	Eidos
2002–4	First Advice
2004–9	Thomas Cook
2009–	Etihad

WHERE THE STREETS HAVE BLUE NAMES

Manchester City Council made the decision to name several streets surrounding Maine Road after the heroes from yesteryear in 1977. The list of names is: Horace Barnes Close, Eric Brook Close, Tommy Browell Close, Sammy Cookson Close, Sam Cowan Close, Billy Meredith Close and Fred Tilson Close. There is also Frank Swift Walk, Billy Meredith Walk and Max Woosnam Walk. An access road, of sorts, was named Joe Mercer Way outside the City of Manchester Stadium.

SUBSTITUTES

The first substitute for Manchester City was Glyn Pardoe for the first match of the 1965/66 season. He remained unused that day, but three games later Roy Cheetham was and became the first City sub to actually play during a match, coming on during a 4–2 win at Wolves. Paul Dickov holds the record for most appearances from the bench, with 67 introductions up to the start of May 2007.

SUNDAY, SUNDAY

With Britain in the grip of strike fever and a three-day working week imposed, the Football League announced a programme of Sunday football for the first time on 20 January 1974. It would be a week later before City played against Nottingham Forest in round four of the FA Cup and duly lost 4–1. It would be a dozen years before they played on a Sunday again, losing 5–4 to Chelsea in the Full

Members' Cup final. The 2001/02 season in Division Two saw the Blues play a record number of Sunday games with ITV Digital seemingly keen to cover every game, and church attendances in Manchester fell sharply. These days it seems odd if there aren't at least ten Sunday games per season.

TV TIMES

The very first televised game from Maine Road was on 15 December 1956 when City lost 3–2 to Wolves in front of just over 30,000 fans. The highlights were featured on BBC Television's *Sports Special* the same evening. The result was symptomatic of the years ahead when for a long time the Blues seemed to freeze in front of the cameras, especially live broadcasts.

In what would be the first of many games televised live from Maine Road featuring the Blues, City lost 2–0 to Chelsea on 4 May 1984. The first live Monday night Premiership fixture on Sky Sports was a 1–1 draw between City and QPR.

TESTIMONIALS

The last testimonial at Maine Road was thoroughly deserved and a crowd of over 25,000 turned out to pay tribute to Paul Lake, whose battle against injury stretched over five long years. Joe Corrigan had a benefit match on 7 November 1979 and must have been bitterly disappointed by the crowd of just 8,104 who turned up to see City beat Werder Bremen 4–0 at Maine Road. Paul Power, Mike Doyle and Colin Bell have all had testimonial games during the 1970s and 1980s but one of the biggest crowds for a tribute match was for Bert Trautmann. Up to 60,000 turned out for the game in 1964 and Maine Road was jam-packed with people eager to pay homage to the legendary German goalkeeper who broke his neck helping City lift the FA Cup in 1956.

TEXACO CUP

Forerunner of the Anglo-Scottish Cup, the Texaco Cup was no more than a series of slightly more competitive friendlies than the usual pre-season fare. The very first games were actually played during the 1971/72 season and the Blues crashed out in round one. The tournament then became pre-season and the next time they entered, the Blues went out in the group stages. City fans have just had to live without the glory of a Texaco Cup triumph. The details are:

Round One

15 September 1971   City 2 (Mellor, Doyle), Airdrie 2
                     Att: 15,033

27 September 1971   Airdrie 2, City 0 Att: 13,700

Group One

3 August 1974   Blackpool 1, City 1 (Tueart)
                    Att: 12,342

6 August 1974   Sheffield United 4, City 2
                    (Summerbee, Law) Att: 9,358

10 August 1974   City 2 (Lee, Tueart), Oldham Athletic 1
                    Att: 13,880

UEFA CUP

City began life in the UEFA Cup, formerly known as the Fairs Cup, in 1972/73 with a home leg against Valencia. The game ended 2–2 with goals from Ian Mellor and Rodney Marsh. The second leg ended the Blues' interest in the tournament with a 2–1 defeat by the Spaniards, with Marsh again finding the back of the net. Four years later in 1976/77 and it was adios, or rather ciao, in the first round, again despite a good home victory, this time over Italian giants Juventus. A solitary goal, courtesy of a Brian Kidd header, was never going to be enough against a cynical side and there were no surprises when the Blues lost 2–0 in Turin to crash out of the competition. The curse continued the following year when Polish side Widzew Lodz held City 2–2 in the first leg and 0–0 in the second, meaning that City were out on the away goals rule.

The fourth UEFA Cup campaign for City was the best, in 1978/79. It was perhaps no coincidence that the first time the club had played the away leg first resulted in success. The Blues ground out a tough 1–1 draw with Dutch side FC Twente and then completed the job with a 3–2 win at Maine Road. Belgian side Standard Liege were put to the sword in the first leg of the second round, losing 4–0 at Maine Road, but clawed back some respectability by winning the second leg 2–0.

Next up were AC Milan in the third round. Fog meant the game was played on the afternoon following the scheduled date but when the action finally began, the Blues went sensationally 2–0 ahead through Power and Kidd. As City headed towards being the first English club to win at the San Siro, Milan fought back to draw 2–2, though City completed the job by thrashing the Italians 3–0 in the second leg. In the quarter-finals crack German outfit Borussia Moenchengladbach earned a 1–1 draw at Maine Road and won 3–1 in the second leg, despite the goal of the game from Kaziu Deyna. The Germans went on to win the UEFA Cup. In 2003 City played their first UEFA Cup qualifier by beating Welsh minnows Total Network Solutions 5–0 and 2–0, before edging past Belgian side Lokeren 3–2 and 1–0. Polish team Groclin Dyskobolia dumped Kevin Keegan's side out on away goals in the next round after a 1–1 draw at the City of Manchester Stadium and a 0–0 draw in Poland. In 2009 the Blues reached the last eight of the competition, losing 3–1 to Hamburg in Germany before winning the return 2–1 only to bow out on aggregate.

THE EUROPA LEAGUE

City embarked on their first Europa League campaign during the 2010/11 season, reaching the last sixteen. City beat FC Timisoara to qualify for the group stages and beat Salzburg home and away, won one and lost one against Lech Poznan as well as drawing twice with Juventus. After seeing off Greek side Aris, the Blues lost to Dynamo Kiev in the round of sixteen, losing 2–0 in the Ukraine and winning the home leg 1–0.

Total record to date:
Pld: 12   W: 7   D: 3   L: 2   F: 18   A: 8

A LOT OF WEATHER
WE'VE BEEN HAVING LATELY

In 1906, City finished the game with Woolwich Arsenal with just six men on the pitch having lost five players from heat exhaustion. With temperatures over 90 degrees

Fahrenheit – this is Manchester, let's not forget – it was no great shock that the Blues lost 4–1. Two days later, the drained players had to play again and went down 9–1 to Everton, but gained revenge in the return at Hyde Road by winning 3–1 in cooler conditions. The famous 4–1 victory over Tottenham in December 1967 was played on a snow-covered, icy Maine Road pitch but such was City's mastery of the surface it was later dubbed 'The Ballet on Ice'.

WAR GAMES

There were many City players who proudly served their country during the Second World War. They are as follows:

Army
Sam Barkas, Harry Brunton, Alex Herd, William Hogan, James Hope, William McLeod, Sam Pearson, Harvey Pritchard, James Rudd, George Smith, Bert Sproston, Frank Swift, Eric Westwood, Thomas Wright and Lewis Woodroffe.

Royal Navy
Albert Emptage and Joe Fagan.

RAF
Jackie Bray, Louis Cardwell, David Davenport, Peter Doherty, Maurice Dunkley, Wilfred Grant, Alf Keeling and manager Wilf Wild.

WEST GORTON

In 1881, after one year of being known as St Mark's of West Gorton, the club became West Gorton (St Mark's) and the humble beginnings of Manchester City were slowly taking shape. The team wore a black kit with a silver Maltese cross on the front – just about as far as you could get from what are believed to be the traditional sky blue colours City would eventually become best known for.

It would prove to be the second of five names for the club and with no real home to call their own, the club's pioneers played matches at Clowes Street, Kirkmanshulme Lane Cricket Club, Queens Road, Pink Bank Lane and Reddish Lane. They stayed as West Gorton for three years before becoming Gorton in 1884.

WE'RE THE FAMOUS MAN CITY AND WE'RE GOING TO WEMBLEY

The Blues have had their fair share of Wembley finals – probably more than many young supporters will realise. The very first time City went to the Twin Towers was in 1926 when Bolton Wanderers beat the Blues 1–0. Seven years later, City again lost, this time to Everton by 3–0. The Blues returned the following season to lift the trophy for the first time, with Fred Tilson grabbing a brace in a 2–1 win over Portsmouth. History repeated itself in 1955 when City first lost to Newcastle 3–1 then returned in 1956 to lift the Cup with a 3–1 win over Birmingham City. In 1969, the Blues beat Leicester City 1–0 with a thunderous strike from Neil Young. A year later, a 2–1 win over West Bromwich Albion secured the League Cup for the very first time. In 1974 City lost 2–1 to Wolves in the League Cup final, but two years later in 1976, Dennis Tueart scored one of the greatest goals the famous old stadium had ever seen – an overhead kick – to clinch a 2–1 win over Newcastle United. City had been to Wembley an impressive four times in seven years.

In 1981 City played there twice in four days, drawing the FA Cup final 1–1 with Spurs and returning the following Thursday to lose 3–2 in one of the most exciting – but ultimately disappointing – finals ever. The only other two occasions the club has played on the lush, green north London turf was an amazing 5–4 defeat to Chelsea in the much-maligned – and unfortunately named – Full Members' Cup final in 1986.

The 1999 play-off final against Gillingham was the club's last appearance at Wembley Stadium for twelve years before the FA Cup semi-final against Manchester United took place in 2011. Having beaten the Reds, City then went on to beat Stoke in the final.

The total record for the Blues at Wembley is:

| Pld: 15 | W: 7 | D: 2 | L: 6 | F: 23 | A: 24 |

TAKING IT TO THE MAX

'Gentleman' Max Woosnam, who joined City from Corinthians in November 1919, was one of the great sportsmen of his era. A Cambridge Blue at golf, tennis and football, he also won a Wimbledon doubles title and was an Olympic gold medalist for tennis. On occasion, Max carried a handkerchief around the pitch to befit his image and the well-groomed superstar of his day was immaculately dressed and respected by all. Liverpool-born Woosnam was a huge success with the City fans and this gifted man was also a powerful defender who captained both City and England. He was also a pioneer of amateurs; being allowed to play with professionals increasing his popularity even more within the game, especially when he took a stand against the Amateur Football Association over the matter. He broke his leg on a fence that surrounded Hyde Road in 1922 and in October 1925 he left for Northwich Victoria, having made a lasting impression on the Blues and on sport the world over. Truly, a one-off.

CAN WE START AGAIN?

The worst-ever start to a league campaign for City was in 1980/81 when eight losses and four draws were recorded from twelve games. The run resulted in Malcolm Allison's sacking and accordingly the next game – unlucky 13 – resulted in a 3–1 victory over Tottenham at Maine Road. To the eternal credit of new manager John Bond, City ultimately finished in twelfth position. Alan Ball presided over nine league defeats and two draws at the start of the 1995/96 campaign and, hardly surprisingly, the Blues were relegated the following May.

THE KIDS ARE ALL RIGHT

The club's youth team has won the coveted FA Youth Cup on two occasions. In 1986 both City and United made it to the two-legged final. The first leg, watched by just 7,602, ended 1–1 at Old Trafford with Paul Lake scoring for City. The second leg at Maine Road was watched by 18,164 partisan City supporters, who roared the young Blues on to a 2–0 win, with goals from Moulden and Boyd. City had previously reached the final in 1978/79 and 1979/80 and then again in 2005/06, but were losers to Millwall, Aston Villa and Liverpool respectively. In 2008, City beat Chelsea over two legs to lift the FA Youth Cup for the second time, drawing 1–1 at Stamford Bridge and winning the return leg of the final 3–1.

FIRSTS

These are City's first results in all competitions:

League

3 September 1892   v Bootle (h)   7–0

FA Cup (qualifying round)

3 October 1891   v Newton Heath (a)   1–5

League Cup

18 October 1960   v Stockport County (h)   3–0

European Cup

18 September 1968   v Fenerbahce (h)   0–0

European Cup Winners' Cup

17 September 1969   v Atletico Bilbao (a)   3–3

UEFA Cup

13 September 1972   v Valencia (h)   2–2

Europa League

19 Aug 2010   v FC Timisoara (a)   1–0

ZENITH DATA SYSTEMS CUP

It's an unfortunate fact of life that the Blues' awful decade from 1980 to 1990 saw the club enter some truly forgettable, awkwardly-named competitions that held little more than embarrassment for the City faithful. The Zenith

Data Systems Cup was such a competition. In 1989 the Blues played three games in a bid to lift a trophy few were interested in, beating Middlesbrough 2–1 at Maine Road and then Sheffield United 2–0 away. Leeds United ended the Blues' interest 2–0 at Elland Road – just as everybody was getting excited! The following year City went out at the first hurdle in a 3–2 defeat at Sheffield Wednesday.

WHO GIVES A TOSS?

The only recorded game involving City decided by the toss of a coin was played in August 1976 during the Tennent-Caledonian Cup – a four-club tournament held in Scotland in which the Blues' opening opponents were Southampton. After the match finished level at 1–1, a penalty shoot-out ensued but the sides were inseparable and ended at 11–11 before the referee instructed the tie to be settled by the old heads or tails method. City skipper Mike Doyle called wrong and the Saints went marching on to the final. City's reward was a third place play-off with Partick Thistle, which they won easily 4–1 in front of a crowd of 35,000.

NOT IN OUR LEAGUE ...

City have played a number of teams no longer in the Football League. Here is a list of sides the Blues have met competitively in the past, yet now play non-league football (as of 2010/11):

Luton Town	(Blue Square Premier)
Wrexham	(Blue Square Premier)
Grimsby Town	(Blue Square Premier)
Mansfield Town	(Blue Square Premier)
Darlington	(Blue Square Premier)

York City	(Blue Square Premier)
Halifax Town	(Evo-Stik Premier League)
Southport	(Blue Square Premier)
Northwich Victoria	(Evo-Stik Premier League)
Cambridge United	(Blue Square Premier)
Newport County	(Blue Square Premier)
Glossop North End	(North West Counties League Premier Division)
Bootle	(North West Counties League Premier Division)
Darwen	(Vodkat League First Division)
Gainsborough Trinity	(Blue Square North)
Loughborough FC	(North Leicestershire Football League)
New Brighton	(Carlsberg West Cheshire Division Two)
South Shields	(STL Northern Football League Division One)

THEY THOUGHT IT WAS ALL OVER ...

Two of the most memorable comebacks for and against City in the past 20 years involved half-time leads of 3–0. In May 1989, City led 3–0 at home to Bournemouth in the penultimate match of the season. Knowing a win would secure promotion, the 30,564 fans inside Maine Road began to celebrate in earnest – but Bournemouth, with nothing but pride to play for fought back to 3–3 with a penalty in the seventh minute of injury time. In February 2004, the Blues then went in at the break trailing 3–0 to Tottenham in an FA Cup fourth round replay at White Hart Lane. Joey Barton was sent off as the teams left the field making the task seem almost impossible. But goals from Sylvain Distin, Paul

Bosvelt, Shaun Wright-Phillips and a last minute winner from Jon Macken completed an incredible turnaround – a 4–3 victory that even the most optimistic City fans could not have dreamed up.

PUB SCORES

You've seen the kind of results in the local free paper – you know the ones, 'Dog and Duck 12, The Swan 7' – well occasionally, those scores happen in professional football, too – here are a selection of pub scores (league games) from City's past:

1894	v Small Heath (a)	2–10
1895	v Lincoln City (h)	11–3
1898	v Darwen (h)	10–0
1902	v Gainsborough (h)	9–0
1919	v Blackburn (h)	8–2
1925	v Burnley (h)	8–3
1925	v Sheffield United (a)	3–8
		(2 days after above result!)
1925	v Bury (a)	5–6
1927	v Swansea (h)	7–4
1933	v WBA (h)	2–7
1938	v Tranmere (a)	9–3
1962	v Wolves (a)	1–8
1964	v Scunthorpe (h)	8–1
1987	v Huddersfield T (h)	10–1

CHAMPIONS!

City have been crowned champions of England on two occasions – here is the final league table for each season:

Division One 1936/37

	Pld	W	D	L	F	A	Pts
Manchester City	42	22	13	7	107	61	57
Charlton Athletic	42	21	12	9	58	49	54
Arsenal	42	18	16	8	80	49	52
Derby County	42	21	7	14	96	90	49
Wolves	42	21	5	16	84	67	47
Brentford	42	18	10	14	82	78	46
Middlesbrough	42	19	8	15	74	71	46
Sunderland	42	19	6	17	89	87	44
Portsmouth	42	17	10	15	62	66	44
Stoke City	42	15	12	15	72	57	42
Birmingham	42	13	15	14	64	60	41
Grimsby Town	42	17	7	18	86	81	41
Chelsea	42	14	13	15	52	55	41
Preston NE	42	14	13	15	56	67	41
Huddersfield T	42	12	15	15	62	64	39
West Brom	42	16	6	20	77	98	38
Everton	42	14	9	19	81	78	37
Liverpool	42	12	11	19	62	84	35
Leeds United	42	15	4	23	60	80	34
Bolton Wanderers	42	10	14	18	43	66	34
Manchester Utd	42	10	12	20	55	78	32
Sheffield Weds	42	9	12	21	53	69	30

Division One 1967/68

	Pld	W	D	L	F	A	Pts
Manchester City	42	26	6	10	86	43	58
Manchester Utd	42	24	8	10	89	55	56
Liverpool	42	22	11	9	71	40	55
Leeds United	42	22	9	11	71	41	53
Everton	42	23	6	13	67	40	52
Chelsea	42	18	12	12	62	68	48
Tottenham H	42	19	9	14	70	59	47
West Brom	42	17	12	13	75	62	46
Arsenal	42	17	10	15	60	56	44
Newcastle United	42	13	15	14	54	67	41
Nottm Forest	42	14	11	17	52	64	39
West Ham United	42	14	10	18	73	69	38
Leicester City	42	13	12	17	64	69	38
Burnley	42	14	10	18	64	71	38
Sunderland	42	13	11	18	51	61	37
Southampton	42	13	11	18	66	83	37
Wolves	42	14	8	20	66	75	36
Stoke City	42	14	7	21	50	73	35
Sheffield Weds	42	11	12	19	51	63	34
Coventry City	42	9	15	18	51	71	33
Sheffield United	42	11	10	21	49	70	32
Fulham	42	10	7	25	56	98	27

A MAN OF HIS POSITION

Eric Brook knew the flanks of Maine Road right down to
the last blade of grass having made 498 appearances for the
Blues in the same outside left position between 1928 and
1939.

INTERNATIONAL BLUES

Several former Manchester City players have gone on to manage national sides. They are:

Peter Doherty	Northern Ireland (1951–2)
Don Revie	England (1974–7)
Mick McCarthy	Republic of Ireland (1996–2002)
Aage Hareide	Norway (2003–8)

CITY'S SHORTEST SEASON

The Blues' shortest ever season was in 1939/40, when, following a 4–3 defeat at Leicester City, a 1–1 draw at home to Bury and a 2–0 win over Chesterfield, the Football League programme was suspended owing to the outbreak of the Second World War. City were in ninth position in Division Two at the time.

JEEPERS KEEPERS

There have been the odd occasions when City keepers have left their goals behind to either add muscle up front or because the situation demanded it. Due to an injured hand, Harry Dowd was forced to play up front when City played Bury in a league game in 1963 and he scored the Blues' only goal during a 1–1 draw. Martyn Margetson climbed off the bench against Torquay in 1990 to play a few manic moments as an emergency striker and who could forget David James' brief cameo as a striker against Middlesbrough in 2005? James is the only keeper to change jerseys for the last 10 minutes, purely as a tactical move and his presence helped win City a late penalty that, if converted, would have put City into the UEFA Cup at Middlesbrough's expense. With many screaming for James to take the penalty, Robbie Fowler lumbered up and saw his attempt saved. The first City keeper to ever score was Charlie Williams in December 1899, when his long punt up field found its way past his opposite number in a 3–1 loss at Sunderland.

FROM OUT OF NOWHERE

City have signed many players who went on to play for the first team after arriving from non-league clubs over the years – here is a team made up of non-league signings:

Bert Trautmann (St Helen's Town)

R. Little (Greenwood)   **M. Woosnam** (Corinthians)
P. Lake (Blue Star)   **C. Sear** (Oswestry)

Billy Meredith (Chirk)   **C. Wilson** (Moss Side)
Billy Lot Jones (Chirk)

P. Sugrue (Nuneaton)   **Tom Johnson** (Dalton Casuals)
Jackie Dyson (Nelson)

ONLY CITY

In 1926, the managerless Blues became the first Manchester side to play at Wembley, losing to Bolton in the FA Cup final. That same season, City recorded the highest-ever

Manchester derby win, a wonderful 6–1 victory at Old Trafford – yet despite all the glory, the Blues were still relegated at the end of the campaign!

BOO BOYS

Some players find themselves getting short shrift from the supporters, whether deserved or not, and here's a few names that have suffered at the hands of the minority of 'boo-boys' over the years – the starred players eventually won the fans over and became crowd favourites:

Joe Corrigan*
Shaun Goater*
Trevor Morley*
Robert Hopkin
Rick Holden
Ian Bowyer
Kevin Bond

ALIAS SMITH AND JONES

If the Smiths' intentions over the years has been to keep up with the Jones', they've done a fine job. The Jones clan clocks in with eight players who had that surname and played for City, while the Smiths just edge it with nine. Seven players with the surname Davies have passed through the club's doors and there have been six Robinsons, five Williams, four Johnsons, four Hills but alas no Partridge and no Peartree.

NIALL QUINN'S DISCO PANTS

The legend of big Niall's disco pants draws its origins from a club tour where the Big Irishman is alleged to have joined supporters for a bit of a bar crawl wearing pants that appeared to be hitched a little on the high side. To the tune 'Here we go' was borne the following chant:

> Niall Quinn's disco pants are the best,
> They go up from his arse to his chest,
> They're better than Adam and the Ants,
> Niall Quinn's, disco pants!

NICKNAMES

Here is a random selection of nicknames for City players over the years – some obvious, some not so:

Boy	Tom Johnson
Spud	Billy Murphy
Nijinsky	Colin Bell
Lee One Pen	Franny Lee
The Goat	Shaun Goater
Buzzer	Mike Summerbee
Inchy	Adrian Heath
Waggy	Dave Wagstaffe
Tommy	Mike Doyle
The Artful Dodger	Peter Beagrie
The Big Irishman	Niall Quinn
Gio	Georgi Kinkladze

ONE FOR THE NEUTRALS

Not including final or semi-final venues, City have had six cup matches replayed on neutral soil after an initial replay failed to settle the tie, winning five and losing one. They are:

1961
Highbury (FA Cup)   v Cardiff 2–0   Att: 24,168

1966
Molineux (FA Cup)   v Everton 0–2   Att: 27,948

1971
Copenhagen (ECWC)   v Gornik Zabrze 3–1   Att: 12,100

1972
Old Trafford (League Cup)   v Walsall 4–0   Att: 13,646

1974
Stamford Bridge (League Cup) v Norwich City 6–1   Att: 6,238

1977
Old Trafford (League Cup)   v Luton Town 3–2   Att: 13,043

CHARITY BEGINS SOMEWHERE ELSE

City have taken part in the FA Charity Shield, now known as the Community Shield, on no less than seven occasions. The first appearance was in 1934, when City lost 4–0 to Arsenal at Highbury in front of 10,888 fans. In 1937, defending league champions City beat Sunderland 2–0 at Maine Road in front of a crowd of 20,000. In October 1956, Manchester United beat FA Cup holders City 1–0 at

Maine Road in front of 30,495 people and in August 1968 defending champs City thrashed West Brom 6–1. A year later and the Blues lost 2–1 at Leeds in front of a crowd just shy of 40,000. City continued to appear in the showpiece fixture in 1972 and 1973, beating Aston Villa and losing to Burnley respectively.

BOXING

Ray Hatton, father of world boxing champion and City fan Ricky 'The Hitman' Hatton, played several reserve games for the Blues during the late 1960s and early '70s before being released. Perhaps his most high profile appearance for the 'stiffs' was during a friendly at Maine Road against Australia where he played alongside Willie Donachie, Dave Connor and Ian Bowyer in a 2–0 victory in front of 7,500 fans. Continuing the boxing theme, Frank Swift occasionally refereed boxing matches and European Lightweight Champion John Murray is also a huge City fan.

FIRST ELEVEN

The very first First XI to play a competitive game for City was: Douglas, Ferguson, Robson, Milne, Whittle, Davidson, Davies, McWhinnie, Weir, Morris and Milarvie. City (then Ardwick) drew 3–3 with Bootle in an Alliance match on September 1891. Prior to that game, the matches played were friendlies and a year later Ardwick became Manchester City with the previous season's feats enough to earn the club a place in Division Two and a first foot on the league ladder. In 1894, the first match of the new season saw no less than ten players make their debuts, with only Fred Dyer having played for City before.

UNDEFEATED

The Blues can only count four seasons when they remained unbeaten at home, with three of those occurring at Hyde Road and only once in 80 years did City remain unbeaten at Maine Road throughout a league campaign. In 1895/96 the Blues won 12 and drew 3 of their 15 home games. In 1904/05 City won 14 and drew 3 times and in 1920/21 City recorded their best-ever home campaign, winning 19 and drawing twice – a record that remains intact 87 years later! The Blues' only undefeated campaign at Maine Road was in 1965/66 when they went on to win the Division Two title having won 14 and drawn 7 of their home games.

CANCEL THE JOLLIES

City once finished a league campaign on 14 June 1947. One player not complaining was City's George Smith who scored all five goals as City beat Newport County 5–1, whose defence had apparently already gone on their holidays.

THAT'LL BE RELEGATION FORM, THEN

City have twice scored a measly 36 league goals in a season and, hardly surprisingly, both campaigns – in 1949/50 and 1986/87 – ended in relegation. That said, in 2006/07 City only scored 29 goals, although a solid defence ensured that relegation was ultimately avoided.

SWINGING SIXTIES

The Blues' busiest season ever was in 1969/70 when they played 60 competitive fixtures. Of those, 42 came in the league, while the other 18 were various cup matches in the League and FA Cup as well as the European Cup Winners' Cup.

BLUES ABROAD

City's first venture into Europe was for an overseas tour in 1910 when they travelled to Germany, Sweden and Denmark, winning four and losing one of their five fixtures. They scored 16 goals and conceded 9. The Blues have hit double figures on five occasions while playing friendly matches on foreign soil. They are:

1938	v Aarhus, Denmark	11–1
1988	v IFK Rundvik, Sweden	10–0
1988	v Lovangers, Sweden	12–0
1990	v Lervik, Norway	10–0
1991	v Skelleften, Sweden	11–1

MARATHON MEN

City and Bolton met no fewer than six times in just over four months during the 1905/06 season. Four of those games were in the Manchester Senior Cup and following three 1–1 draws Bolton finally edged the tie 1–0 in the third replay. City at least had the last laugh by completing a league double of 3–1 wins over the Trotters.

BLUE MOON LYRICS

Blue Moon, you saw me standing alone,
Without a dream in my heart,
Without a love of my own.

Blue Moon, you knew just what I was there for,
You heard me saying a prayer for,
Someone I could really care for.

Then suddenly they'll appear before me,
The only one my arms could ever hold,
I heard someone whisper 'Please adore me,'
And when I looked my moon had turned to gold.

Blue Moon, now I'm no longer alone,
I have a dream in my heart,
I have a love of my own.

© Rodgers & Hart

BOYS IN BLUE LYRICS

City – Manchester City
We are the lads who are playing to win
City, the Boys in Blue will never give in
Football is the game that we all live for
Saturday is the day we play the game
Everybody have to pull together
And together we will stand
Even if we're playing down at Maine Road
Or if we play a million miles away
There will always be a loyal fan behind us
To cheer us on our way
City – Manchester City
We are the lads who are playing to win
City – the Boys in Blue will never give in
Blue and white we play together
We will carry on forever more
Maybe in another generation
When other lads have come to take our place
They'll carry on the glory of the City
Keeping City in the place
City – Manchester City
We are the lads who are playing to win
City – the Boys in Blue will never give in
City – the Boys in Blue will never give in
City – the Boys in Blue will never give in.

ONE FLU OVER THE OWLS' NEST

The only recorded opening match of the season to be postponed was in August 1957 when Sheffield Wednesday's squad was decimated by a flu outbreak and the game had to be re-arranged for 9 October, when the Blues triumphed 2–0 and celebrated with a cup of Lemsip – just in case.

GET WITH THE PROGRAMME

City's first matchday programme was published in September 1898 and grandly entitled *The Official Programme*. Containing info on all Manchester clubs, it was more of a football weekly than a dedicated Blue bible and it wasn't until 1903 that City published their own *Blue and White* matchday programme – a title that lasted more than 50 years until it disappeared for a while in 1954. Today, Ignition Publications produce the matchday programme and have won several awards in recent years due to the quality of their product.

DARK CITY – THE MAINE ROAD NIGHTMARES

It would be foolish to pretend that City's tenure at Maine Road has been all sweetness and light over the years. Indeed, it is an unfortunate fact of life that part of being a Blue is sufferance, turmoil and angst – it is perhaps the agony endured in the line of duty that has made City fans into the most patient, humorous in the land.

So much has happened within the walls of Maine Road and on that rectangular field of dreams that should not be brushed under the carpet or forgotten when the gates were locked for the final time – events that many fans witnessed, but could scarcely believe were actually happening before their very eyes. The legends and myths that are stained into the walls of the club lie thick and heavy and they began before a ball was even kicked on the ground.

When a patch of waste ground was purchased for around £5,000 in 1922, legend has it that a gypsy encampment was ordered off the common so the builders could begin preparing the foundations of City's new home. In time honoured fashion – so the story goes – the furious travellers issued a curse that the new tenants would never enjoy success at the ground. Of course, that never happened and the club won a lot of silverware over the years.

The worst day for most City fans was when Luton Town relegated the Blues from the top flight for the first time in seventeen years. The ghastly sight of David Pleat skipping onto the pitch as the final whistle blew is a difficult memory to erase, however hard one tries, and the football played at Maine Road from 1983 to 1989 was equally forgettable.

Paul Lake, that most graceful footballer cut down in his prime, falling innocuously in a clash with Aston Villa's Tony Cascarino, is another awful memory. Anyone who witnessed the same player swallow his tongue during a home game with Leicester in 1987 could never forget the moment when it looked like the talented utility player was going to die on the pitch. Swift action by the medical team ensured that didn't happen and Lake recovered and returned to action within days.

HONOURS

First Division (old format)
Champions 1937, 1968
Runners-up 1904, 1921, 1977

**Second Division (old format), First Division/
Championship (new format)**
Champions 1899, 1903, 1910, 1928, 1947, 1966, 2002
(7 times, record holders)
Runners-up 1896, 1951, 1989, 2000
Second Division (new format)
Play-off winners 1999

FA Cup
Winners 1904, 1934, 1956, 1969, 2011
Runners-up 1926, 1933, 1955, 1981

League Cup
Winners 1970, 1976
Runners-up 1974

European Cup Winners' Cup
Winners 1970

Charity Shield
Winners 1937, 1968, 1972
Runners-up 1934, 1956, 1969, 1973

Full Members' Cup
Runners-up 1986

FOR THE RECORD

Here is a list of notable landmarks in the Blues' history:

Record League victory
11–3 v Lincoln City (23 March 1895)

Record FA Cup victory
12–0 v Liverpool Stanley (4 October 1890)

Record League defeat
1–9 v Everton FC (3 September 1906)

Record FA Cup defeat
0–6 v Preston North End (January 1897)

Highest attendance
84,569 v Stoke City (3 March 1934)

Most League appearances
561 + 3 sub, Alan Oakes 1958–76

Most appearances overall
668 + 4 sub, Alan Oakes 1958–76

Most goals scored overall
178, Eric Book 1928–40

Most goals scored in a season
38, Tommy Johnson 1928/29

Record transfer fee paid
£32.5 million to Real Madrid for Robinho, September 2008

Record transfer fee received
£21 million from Chelsea for Shaun Wright-Phillips, July 2005

THEY SAID IT ...

'In all my years I've been a manager it's the first time I've seen one of my sides play so badly and then ended up taking a rollicking for it.'

Joe Mercer tells Malcolm Allison about Mike Summerbee's reverse psychology (1968)

'In the end, I left before I could do any long-term harm. I regret not leaving the City fans with a positive image of me – instead, they must be bewildered.'

Steve Coppell laments his brief time as City manager (1997)

THE GREATEST DERBY GAMES

City v United – the greatest derby of them all – relive some of our best days taking on that lot from over the road . . .

Premiership
9 November 2002
City 3, United 1
The last ever Maine Road derby – the 137th meeting between the Manchester rivals – was always going to be an emotional day for the supporters and players. The one remit the fans demanded from the Blues was a victory – not too much to ask for! City hadn't enjoyed success in this fixture since September 1989 and began the game impressively with crisp passing and neat, effective build-up play. It took only six minutes for Keegan's men to take a deserved lead. Nicolas Anelka left Rio Ferdinand for dead as he raced towards United's goal. He intelligently slipped the ball to Shaun Goater who sent a low drive in from just inside the

box. Fabien Barthez could only parry the shot into Anelka's path and he made no mistake from six yards out. It was the perfect start and the home fans went crazy.

A strangely muted United showed why they can never be written off by equalising two minutes later through Ole Gunnar Solskjaer who poked a Giggs cross home, much to the chagrin of Peter Schmeichel. The Blues started again and slowly began to take command and in the 26th minute, they retook the lead. Goater chased an over-hit pass but Gary Neville appeared to be in complete control of the ball. The City striker continued approaching Neville who appeared in two minds as to what to do. Goater stole the ball from him and angled in on the United goal before expertly rolling the ball by the goalkeeper for a goal out of absolutely nothing.

The City fans wasted no time in making Neville's life a misery and he would endure ironic chants and cheers until the final whistle. City led 2–1 at the break and a noisy Maine Road waited to see what was in store for the second period. Things were going to plan so far but victory over United had become so rare, few dared dream that things would stay they way they were. Yet within five minutes of the restart, City were 3–1 up. Berkovic, in complete control of the midfield, fed Goater in the box and he delicately lifted the ball over the onrushing Barthez for his 100th goal in City colours. Needless to say, the ground erupted yet again.

The Blues should have added more as they totally outplayed the Reds in a comprehensive and fully deserved win. It was only as the referee blew for time that the realisation began to set in that City had actually beaten United in the final derby to ever take place at Maine Road. It was a fantastic day to be a Blue.

Division One
25 September 1989
City 5, United 1

Perhaps the favourite Maine Road match of all-time was the day Mel Machin's young City side tore the heart out of Alex Ferguson's pitiful Reds with a fearsome attacking display. The Blues were simply irresistible on the day and would have turned over far better sides than United, such was the level of excellence. Everything went right for City from start to finish and it was difficult for the fans of either side to absorb what was happening in front of them, yet the game began with ugly scenes in the North Stand as around a hundred United supporters seated among the home fans began fighting, causing the teams to be taken off for several minutes. The incident seemed to fire the Blues even more and they quickly took command of the game and soon opened the scoring with David White's pulled-back cross being converted by David Oldfield. A minute later and it was 2–0 as Paul Lake's shot was parried by Jim Leighton into the path of Trevor Morley who scrambled home.

Two became three when Steve Redmond sent Oldfield clear down the right flank. He looked up and whipped in a perfect cross for Ian Bishop to score with a wonderful diving header. Three down at the break, the United fans were quiet as lambs as they contemplated what fresh horrors the second half might bring. It was the Reds, however, who drew first blood with an acrobatic Mark Hughes goal flying past Paul Cooper within minutes of the action resuming. Danny Wallace then sent in a low drive that Cooper did well to save as United enjoyed their best spell. It was only a temporary blip as Lake set up an easy fourth for Oldfield on 58 minutes. The nail chewing stopped and the home support began to enjoy the afternoon again by taunting the Reds' fans in the Platt Lane.

The goal of the game followed four minutes later with a flowing move that once again sent Maine Road into raptures. Bishop sent a long pass out to White on the right and the flying winger crossed the ball immediately for Andy Hinchcliffe to rocket a header in to make it 5–1. The visiting support turned en masse to exit the ground only to find the gates closed – there was no escape! Some began to chant 'Fergie Out!' but, of course, destiny was to be far kinder to the United boss in future years. There were no further goals, despite almost 30 minutes more of play but nobody cared. The annihilation was complete and what would be the biggest ever derby win for City at Maine Road remains a cherished day for Blues everywhere.

Division One
6 November 1971
City 3, United 3
Now under the leadership of Malcolm Allison who had been promoted to team manager as Joe Mercer moved 'upstairs', City, in third spot, were once again seriously challenging for the league championship for the visit of cross-town rivals United. It was a period when the Reds couldn't beat City home or away. The game, packed with the stars of the era – Summerbee, Best, Lee, Law and Bell – went to form early on with Franny Lee converting a penalty after he'd been pulled down by Tommy O'Neil putting the Blues, who had begun impressively, 1–0 up. Then followed a moment of pure theatre as Lee complained that George Best had taken a dive to earn a free kick. He protested to the referee before taking a mock dive into the mud to illustrate his gripe.

United fought back to lead 2–1 with 17-year-old Sammy McIlroy making a fantastic start to his career with the Reds, but Colin Bell made it 2–2 as the game swung from one end to the other. There were plenty of niggles all over the pitch and referee Ray Tinkler cautioned three players during the game but missed several other controversial moments that could have worn the lead in his pencil down to a stub. An already classic derby match took a dramatic swing when John Aston saw his shot deflected into the Blues' net for 3–2 with minutes to play. It looked like the Reds, who had won at Maine Road 4–3 the previous May, were about to severely dent City's championship ambitions but with seconds left, Mike Summerbee sent in a powerful drive that rocketed past Alex Stepney for a point-saving goal. A draw was a fair result to a cracking Manchester derby and a 3–1 win at Old Trafford – their fifth victory there in succession – later in the season made City top dogs in the city yet again.

THEY SAID IT …

'Are you watching Alan Brazil?!'

The City players celebrate promotion at Blackburn in May 2000 with a special message to one of their biggest detractors, Sky commentator and Ipswich fan Alan Brazil

'The only time I want to see him miserable is after I've taken City to Old Trafford.'

Kevin Keegan on Sir Alex Ferguson (2001)

'People will remember 99 more than 100 and he'll probably get another chance to star in an advert for ice cream or something.'

Kevin Keegan makes light of Stuart Pearce's last career appearance penalty miss (2002)

CITY'S COMPLETE LEAGUE RECORD
1892–2011

C – Champions · P – Promoted · R – Relegated

Season	Div	Pld	W	D	L	F	A	Pts	Pos	
1892/3	D2	22	9	3	10	45	40	21	5	
1893/4	D2	28	8	2	18	47	71	18	13	
1894/5	D2	30	14	3	13	82	72	31	9	
1895/6	D2	30	21	4	5	63	38	46	2	
1896/7	D2	30	12	8	10	58	50	32	6	
1897/8	D2	30	15	9	6	66	36	39	3	
1898/9	D2	34	23	6	5	92	35	52	1	C
1899/1900	D1	34	13	8	13	50	44	34	7	
1900/1	D1	34	13	6	15	48	58	32	11	
1901/2	D1	34	11	6	17	42	58	28	18	R
1902/3	D2	34	25	4	5	95	29	54	1	C
1903/4	D1	34	19	6	9	71	45	44	2	
1904/5	D1	34	20	6	8	66	37	46	3	
1905/6	D1	38	19	5	14	73	54	43	5	
1906/7	D1	38	10	12	16	53	77	32	17	
1907/8	D1	38	16	11	11	62	54	43	3	
1908/9	D1	38	15	4	19	67	69	34	19	R
1909/10	D2	38	23	8	7	81	40	54	1	C
1910/11	D1	38	9	13	16	43	58	31	17	
1911/12	D1	38	13	9	16	56	58	35	15	
1912/13	D1	38	18	8	12	53	37	44	6	
1913/14	D1	38	14	8	16	51	53	36	13	
1914/15	D1	38	15	13	10	49	39	43	5	
1919/20	D1	42	18	9	15	71	62	45	7	
1920/1	D1	42	24	6	12	70	50	54	2	
1921/2	D1	42	18	9	15	65	70	45	10	
1922/3	D1	42	17	11	14	50	49	45	8	
1923/4	D1	42	15	12	15	54	71	42	11	
1924/5	D1	42	17	9	16	76	68	43	10	

Season	Div	Pld	W	D	L	F	A	Pts	Pos	
1925/6	D1	42	12	11	19	89	100	35	21	R
1926/7	D2	42	22	10	10	108	61	54	3	
1927/8	D2	42	25	9	8	100	59	59	1	C
1928/9	D1	42	18	9	15	95	86	45	8	
1929/30	D1	42	19	9	14	91	81	47	3	
1930/1	D1	42	18	10	14	75	70	46	8	
1931/2	D1	42	13	12	17	83	73	38	14	
1932/3	D1	42	16	5	21	68	71	37	16	
1933/4	D1	42	17	11	14	65	72	45	5	
1934/5	D1	42	20	8	14	82	67	48	4	
1935/6	D1	42	17	8	17	68	60	42	9	
1936/7	D1	42	22	13	7	107	61	57	1	C
1937/8	D1	42	14	8	20	80	77	36	21	R
1938/9	D2	42	21	7	14	96	72	49	5	
1946/7	D2	42	26	10	6	78	35	62	1	C
1947/8	D1	42	15	12	15	52	47	42	10	
1948/9	D1	42	15	15	12	47	51	45	7	
1949/50	D1	42	8	13	21	36	68	29	21	R
1950/1	D2	42	19	14	9	89	61	52	2	P
1951/2	D1	42	13	13	16	58	61	39	15	
1952/3	D1	42	14	7	21	72	87	35	20	
1953/4	D1	42	14	9	19	62	77	37	17	
1954/5	D1	42	18	10	14	76	69	46	7	
1955/6	D1	42	18	10	14	82	69	46	4	
1956/7	D1	42	13	9	20	78	88	35	18	
1957/8	D1	42	22	5	15	104	100	49	5	
1958/9	D1	42	11	9	22	64	95	31	20	
1959/60	D1	42	17	3	22	78	84	37	16	
1960/1	D1	42	13	11	18	79	90	37	13	
1961/2	D1	42	17	7	18	78	81	41	12	
1962/3	D1	42	10	11	21	58	102	31	21	R
1963/4	D2	42	18	10	14	84	66	46	6	
1964/5	D2	42	16	9	17	63	62	41	11	
1965/6	D2	42	22	15	5	76	44	59	1	C

Season	Div	Pld	W	D	L	F	A	Pts	Pos	
1966/7	D1	42	12	15	15	43	52	39	15	
1967/8	D1	42	26	6	10	86	43	58	1	C
1968/9	D1	42	15	10	17	64	55	40	13	
1969/70	D1	42	16	11	15	55	48	43	10	
1970/1	D1	42	12	17	13	47	42	41	11	
1971/2	D1	42	23	11	8	77	45	57	4	
1972/3	D1	42	15	11	16	57	60	41	11	
1973/4	D1	42	14	12	16	39	46	40	14	
1974/5	D1	42	18	10	14	54	54	46	8	
1975/6	D1	42	16	11	15	64	46	43	8	
1976/7	D1	42	21	14	7	60	34	56	2	
1977/8	D1	42	20	12	10	74	51	52	4	
1978/9	D1	42	13	13	16	58	56	39	15	
1979/80	D1	42	12	13	17	43	66	37	17	
1980/1	D1	42	14	11	17	56	59	39	12	
1981/2	D1	42	15	13	14	49	50	58	10	
1982/3	D1	42	13	8	21	47	70	47	20	R
1983/4	D2	42	20	10	12	66	48	70	4	
1984/5	D2	42	21	11	10	66	40	74	3	P
1985/6	D1	42	11	12	19	43	57	45	15	
1986/7	D1	42	8	15	19	36	57	39	21	R
1987/8	D2	44	19	8	17	80	60	65	9	
1988/9	D2	46	23	13	10	77	53	82	2	P
1989/90	D1	38	12	12	14	43	52	48	14	
1990/1	D1	38	17	11	10	64	53	62	5	
1991/2	D1	42	20	10	12	61	48	70	5	
1992/3	PR	42	15	12	15	56	51	57	9	
1993/4	PR	42	9	18	15	38	49	45	16	
1994/5	PR	42	12	13	17	53	64	49	17	
1995/6	PR	38	9	11	18	33	58	38	18	R
1996/7	D1	46	17	10	19	59	60	61	14	
1997/8	D1	46	12	12	22	56	57	48	22	R
1998/9	D2	46	22	16	8	69	33	82	3	P
1999/2000	D1	46	26	11	9	78	40	89	2	P

Season	Div	Pld	W	D	L	F	A	Pts	Pos	
2000/1	PR	38	8	10	20	41	65	34	18	R
2001/2	D1	46	31	6	9	108	52	99	1	C
2002/3	PR	38	15	6	17	47	54	51	9	
2003/4	PR	38	9	14	15	55	54	41	16	
2004/5	PR	38	13	13	12	47	39	52	8	
2005/6	PR	38	13	4	21	43	48	43	15	
2006/7	PR	38	11	9	18	29	44	42	14	
2007/8	PR	38	15	10	13	45	53	55	9	
2008/9	PR	38	15	5	18	58	50	50	10	
2009/10	PR	38	18	13	7	73	45	67	5	
2010/11	PR	38	21	8	9	60	33	71	3	

THEY SAID IT …

'It's just like watching Brazil!'

The City fans – originators of the chant, not Barnsley – at Oxford as Kinkladze orchestrates a 4–1 win (1997)

'We went to Kinky's first game and came away thinking, "well, we're either going to be in the European Cup or in Division Four in five years."'

Noel Gallagher (1997)

'We could qualify for Europe this season or we could get relegated – that's why I support City.'

Noel Gallagher highlights the source of City fans' addiction (2000)

COMPLETE RECORD OF CITY MANAGERS

Lawrence Furniss	1889–93	First manager of League era
Joshua Parlby	1893–5	
Sam Ormerod	1895–1902	
Tom Maley	1902–6	
Harry Newbould	1906–12	
Ernest Mangnall	1912–24	
David Ashworth	1924–5	
Peter Hodge	1926–32	
Wilf Wild	1932–46	
Sam Cowan	1946–7	
Jock Thomson	1947–50	
Les McDowall	1950–63	
George Poyser	1963–5	
Joe Mercer	1965–71	
Malcolm Allison	1971–3	
Johnny Hart	1973	
Ron Saunders	1973–4	
Tony Book	1974–9	
Malcolm Allison	1979–80	
John Bond	1980–3	
John Benson	1983	
Billy McNeill	1983–6	
Jimmy Frizzell	1986–7	
Mel Machin	1987–9	
Howard Kendall	1989–90	
Peter Reid	1990–3	Player-manager
Brian Horton	1993–5	
Alan Ball	1995–6	
Steve Coppell	1996	Shortest reign
Frank Clark	1996–8	
Joe Royle	1998–2001	
Kevin Keegan	2001–5	

Stuart Pearce	2005–7
Sven-Goran Eriksson	2007–8
Mark Hughes	2008–9
Roberto Mancini	2009–

THEY SAID IT …

'Don't worry lads, I've had a word with the groundsman and he's going to water the pitch this afternoon.'
Malcolm Allison before the 1970 ECWC final in Vienna – an hour before about a year's worth of rain fell

ACKNOWLEDGEMENTS

Thanks for buying this updated and revised edition of *The Man City Miscellany* – it means the first version was well-received and probably sold fairly well, too! I'd just like to thank my wife Sarah and my beautiful children Harry, Jaime and Chrissie. I love you all and promise to make up the lost hours spent on projects like this. Thanks to Michelle Tilling, my editor at The History Press for all her patience over the years with my tardiness. Thanks to The Goat for the foreword – much appreciated Shaun! That's pretty much it for this one as most of the hard work was done by Yours Truly – for facts and figures from elsewhere, thanks as well. You know who you are.

David Clayton, Manchester 2011

Other titles published by The History Press

Man City 50 Classic Matches . . . and some to forget!
David Clayton
978-07524-5559-4
From the first game ever played at Maine Road in 1923, to the last in 2003, and from belters at the City of Manchester Stadium to Wembley classics, relegation deciders and thrilling derbies against bitter rivals Manchester United, this book has all the drama you could ever want, and more if you can bear it.

Once in a Blue Moon
Life, Love and Manchester City
Steve Worthington
978-07524-5621-8
Once in a Blue Moon is the story of one man's never-ending affair with Manchester City. Be it playing, watching or managing, Steve 'Worthy' Worthington's life in football has never been easy. Join him in a vivid journey that takes you into the beating heart of 1960s and '70s working class Manchester: through five decades of football, music and people, via the eyes and ears of an everyday bloke who turned constant failure into a triumph.

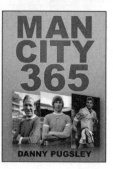

Man City 365
Danny Pugsley
978-07524-5782-6
Man City 365 chronicles, in a day-by-day account, the most significant events and landmarks from every day of the year. Charting classic matches, records, signings, and the most beloved players to the downright bizarre, the book provides a fascinating and often humorous insight and testament to the club and its place in the footballing world.

Visit our website and discover thousands of other History Press books.

www.thehistorypress.co.uk